BLESSED
Beyond
MEASURE

To order additional copies of this book, contact:

www.tomhillwebsite.com

*To my wonderful, loving, and
supportive wife, Betty,*

*who believed in me before I believed
in myself.*

ACKNOWLEDGMENTS

Thanks to the most loving and caring family ever—absolutely blessed beyond measure with each of you. Terri and Mickey, your impact has been huge. To my colleague, Gary Baker: you've touched my life in so many ways—keep soaring my friend! To an amazing writer and friend, Russell Irwin: you are the man. Many thanks to my high school teacher, Oliver Barnard: you helped a young and naïve farm boy grow; to my first RE/MAX partner, Howard McPherson, who gave me a chance that made all the difference; to Jim Brown, a great supporter and friend—way to go "Gymbeaux"; to the late Jim Rohn, who taught me to believe, to dare to dream—I believed you; and to my friends Tim Cross and Doug Damon, who are touching so many lives, keep making a difference. A special thanks to the team, Jeanette Littleton, Kathy Baker, and Kevin Williamson, for your professional expertise and touch. And last, but by no means least: many have contributed to the reality behind my well-known statement "blessed beyond measure"— I love and thank each of you.

CONTENTS

FOREWORD

Recently I met with a twenty-four-year-old about what he wanted to do with his life. He was still in school finishing up a business degree, but he didn't know what he was going to do with it. I asked him what he really wanted to do with his life.

The young man lit up and spoke about his love for flying. Ever since he was a kid he loved the idea of flying. He didn't care whether he was a pilot, a flight attendant, an aviation mechanic, or the custodian who cleans airplane bathrooms, this young man wanted to be around planes.

I asked what was holding him back from doing exactly that.

He answered, "I am too old."

He's twenty-four years old. Too old, he thinks, to do what he loves.

Perhaps you're wondering what this young man, his excuse, this book, and your life have in common? My friend, it's the stories and the excuses we tell ourselves that determine how well we live up to the fullness of our potential. Our excuses hold us back professionally, relationally, and in every facet of life.

It may be that "too old" isn't the excuse you make. I wonder, though, if you've ever said: "I am too young, too rich, too poor, too broken, too unknown, too unskilled, too unworthy, too untalented, too unconnected, too busy, too set in my ways to make the required changes in my life to author a legacy of significance."

If you face challenges that seem to be grounding you, *Blessed Beyond Measure* is certain to free you from excuse and liberate you to make a difference. I've respected Dr. Tom Hill my entire professional life. After reading this book, you'll know why.

Tom is a remarkably successful entrepreneur, but that's not what most attracts me to him. Instead, it is how he lives his life, continually pushes himself to grow, and chooses daily to impact others. He cares genuinely for people and wants to see them thrive. Tom is extremely generous to those he meets, and I've witnessed firsthand how he treats everyone from the CEO to the coffee shop waitress as if they are the most important person in the world. For Tom, *they are.*

He also enjoys an outstanding family. Tom's a wonderful husband, dad, and grandfather. He and his wife, Betty, continue to model what a vibrant, loving relationship looks like in action.

Remarkably, Tom still finds time to be an airplane pilot, marathon runner, mountain climber, skydiver, prolific reader, writer, speaker, and seeker.

Blessed Beyond Measure unites Tom's purpose to make a profound and positive difference in as many lives as possible with his own life story proving the benefit of what he teaches. Many authors eloquently talk the talk, but Dr. Tom Hill boldly walks the walk. This book is his road map to guide the rest of us forward with him.

Read this book for enjoyment. You will be blessed immeasurably by the wow and wonder of Tom's story and the humor and profundity of his storytelling. Read this book for instruction. You will hurdle over excuses active in your life. Read this book to imagine a life of even greater significance than you've dreamed. Read this book to discern how you can change the world through your life.

Blessed Beyond Measure will inspire you through the incredible life of Dr. Tom Hill. Even more importantly, after reading this book you'll be inspired and equipped to start soaring in your own life.

Buckle your seatbelt and get ready for the flight of a lifetime.

—John O'Leary
www.RisingAbove.com

CHAPTER 1

SOARING

34 . . . 35 . . . 36 . . . NOSE UP, AND WE WERE OFF.

Thirty-seven seconds—really amazing! It could have been the two-seater Cessna 150 at its 1,500 lb. capacity load, or 650,000 lbs. on 32 wheels of the fully loaded U.S. Air Force C5A Galaxy . . . at maximum load, lifting off the runway to begin climbing toward cruising altitude always requires the same 37 seconds. The ultimate purpose of a runway is disconnection. It is limited real estate, which essentially means limited time. You want liftoff and you've got to get there quickly. I already knew our transatlantic jet was stuffed full with passengers and baggage. But, just making sure, the rotation test is always fun.

Simply speaking, "rotation" is the point at which the nose of the plane rotates upward and actually lifts the aircraft off the ground. The forward speed necessary before initiating rotation is estimated from simple physics, considering the aircraft's wing area, its center of mass (load distribution), and environmental conditions, such as air temperature (cold air is denser and hot air thinner), wind speed and direction, moisture on the runway, and so forth.

The calculated factors inform a pilot of the critical speed (rotation speed) for creating an angle of attack, taking the plane from parallel to the ground to a point of lift—generally around 15 degrees. The angle of attack is all about how much wind is going over the wings and how much wind beneath them. If it takes longer for air to pass over the upper surfaces of the wing, more lift is created pushing up against the lower side of the wings. And, depending on the load, sufficient lift to escape the confines of gravity will occur between 30 and 37 seconds from the onset of the takeoff roll down the runway.

Calculation ... critical speed ... angle of attack ... liftoff ... there are no passive descriptors related to getting a plane off the ground. And if you do any flying, each of these things (quite literally) impacts your life. Of course, you are not making worrisome mathematical calculations while traveling down the runway. You trust the data correlations on the charts attached to the preflight briefing package for the aircraft you're flying. And it is good to know your trust is based on computations that are measurable and precise.

Whether as pilot or passenger, I have flown them all. Accounting for all-important factors and bringing them together, no timepiece is more exact than point of forward thrust to liftoff, and no achievement so sure as *airborne*.

Dallas descended rapidly into monochromatic patchwork geometry. The earthy tones were notably warmer than those surrounding Lambert International in St. Louis, the sight of our original departure hours earlier. The next time we touched down we would be on another continent. Betty, my wife of thirty-one years, and I were headed to Heathrow—London, England. We had just taken off from DFW. Of course, we were the ones who ascended as Dallas stayed put. But it never appears that way from the window of a passenger seat on a large commercial jetliner.

Now, from the cockpit of a small aircraft, that's another thing. As a pilot, peering over the control panel and through the windshield while disconnecting with earth and heading toward the clouds, there is no illusion—no thought but that I am in control and going skyward. You feel everything in the smaller craft and you imagine more, maybe even wind in your hair. That is how free it feels. Commercial airliners are more routine, more of a point A to point B experience.

I squeezed Betty's hand. When she looked at me, I nodded toward the window. She leaned across me and looked out.

"Love Field," I whispered in her ear.

She sat back in her seat and looked at me with one of those "I wish you'd wipe that smile off your face" playful glares. Then she closed her eyes and shook her head.

Outside the small oval window and far beneath our American Airlines flight 1101 were the sprawling suburbs of the Dallas/Fort Worth area. And somewhere in all that real estate was Love Field, the site of our one and only flight trauma.

The ordeal happened when we were flying to Dallas with our son-in-law, Mickey. By no action of mine, the RPMs began increasing. I pulled the throttle back and nothing happened. I quickly realized the linkage to the carburetor had broken or come loose. The engine was wide open and I could do nothing about it. I called Air Traffic Control (ATC) and told them the situation.

"What do you want?" they asked.

I didn't have to ponder the question.

"I want the longest runway in Dallas," I answered. They gave me Love Field.

After shutting down or diverting all commercial and private air traffic, they guided me in to an 8,000-foot runway (I typically only needed 2,500). We were going about one hundred and eighty miles per hour, three to four times the normal landing speed.

"How much fuel do you have on board?" ATC asked me. I knew what this meant. They wanted to know how many fire trucks to have waiting for us. The next question was even more sobering: "How many souls on board?"

This was all spoken in the typical aviation vernacular. But Betty was sitting behind me hearing the conversation through a headset and to her there was nothing typical about the questions whatsoever. When she heard the word "souls" in the last question, her interpretation was, "We're dead!" She did not react. She did not say a word. She just sat there thinking . . . knowing . . . *We're dead!*

The process of flying ingrains many things in a pilot—things that are not at all dramatic. They are, in fact, essentially routine. If we were to list them in order of importance on a page, DISCIPLINES would be the title at the top. Number one would be: *Checklist.* Everything starts and ends with a checklist. After years of flying, I've found a daily checklist is as much a part of my way of life as getting dressed. A pilot leaves nothing to memory. A checklist alone removes 90 percent of the possibility of human error.

Many pilots have crashed because they have run out of fuel. Running out of fuel in an airplane! How does that happen? Why? A checklist makes such a thing impossible.

Other pilots have crashed by forgetting to disengage ground gear that holds the yoke in place and prevents flaps and ailerons from moving in the wind when parked. They get up to speed for takeoff and crash because they cannot control the plane—the flaps and ailerons are locked in place. Shocking stuff, but it happens, all due to omission of the simple discipline of a checklist.

Another thing that becomes second nature when you are piloting aircraft is knowing what plan B is . . . and maybe plan C! You cannot always control everything. Something can certainly go wrong that no list would protect against. Our situation heading into Love Field fell into that category. I'd logged more than three thousand hours of flying—all piston-powered, single-engine planes—without one scary incident. The checklist had served me well. But on that day the one in ten thousand happened. Even so, I knew the odds were in my favor, so my plan B was simple: stay calm, focus, and execute.

The touchdown was smooth. Using what is called a dead-stick landing, I shut off the engine and shut off the gas. At the end of the runway we coasted up to ten fire trucks, five ambulances, and three police cars. Plan B had worked.

When we rolled to a stop, I turned around to give Betty a high five. She stared at me for a second, then threw her hands in the air and began screaming bloody murder! When she was certain, *We're dead*, she had accepted it and sat quietly. Alive with a moment's processing, she completely lost it! For the return to St. Louis she left the small plane, private flying to Mickey and me and flew home commercial.

It seems like flight has always been part of my life. But the relationship actually began when I was nine years old. On an otherwise ordinary day my Uncle Howard visited our farm in northern Missouri in a rented canvas-covered plane. It was a tandem—two seats, pilot in front and passenger behind—with a 65-horse-powered continental engine. Howard Cole was a U.S. Army Air Corps pilot, and just hearing him offer to take my six-year old sister, Karen, and me for a ride was the thrill of a lifetime at that point.

Strapped into the lone passenger seat with my little sister, I was mesmerized as we circled the farm. By the time we landed, poor Karen was covered in the former contents of my belly, and even though I lost my lunch, I was still smitten with the fascination of flight.

Six years later, when I was fifteen, flying became part of my life in a big way. This was during the late 1940s and my father was a turkey farmer. I don't recall many details of turkey farming, and I don't know anything about the genetics involved in turkey breeding. But I do know Dad invented a turkey—literally.

Soon afterward his new kind of turkey "took off," so to speak, and not in the usual slow, clumsy way of turkeys, but fast and high-flying.

His business, Hill's Hatchery, became known for this special breed of turkey he invented, and the farm grew to a hundred thousand turkeys a year. Day-old poults had to be delivered all over the Midwest and beyond.

When delivering by ground became unmanageable, he did what any right-minded farmer in the middle of nowhere would do: he bought a Cessna 170, cleared an airstrip on our land, and had my older brother, Roger, and I flight trained in a Piper Cub.

To my delight, ten hours of flight time with an instructor was enough to get a student license and fly solo—no passengers. It took another thirty hours or so to qualify for the flight test.

Before we knew it, both Roger and I had a private VFR (Visual Flight Rules) pilot's license and a new job. We took the back seats out of the Cessna, loaded it with turkeys, and began sharing flight time to the Carolinas, Texas, the Dakotas, eastern Colorado, Arkansas, and Tennessee. Dad got as far as his student license, but something happened—we don't know what—and he never got in a plane again. He totally depended on us to fly for him.

Having a plane to make deliveries might sound highfalutin, but this was a pretty low-budget operation. We kept the plane on the farm and had no runway lights. When we arrived home late at night from a delivery, we would swoop in low over the house—low enough to wake up Mom and Dad (two teenagers swooping in the dark of night with no instrumentation, mind you). They would get up, come outside, and turn the car lights on toward the grass runway so we could see where to land. Often cows would be on the runway, and we would have to swoop in even lower—ten to fifteen feet over their heads—to scare them away so we could land.

It might also seem pretty sophisticated for two teenagers to fly a plane as a part-time job. But we never thought of it that way. It was just what we had to do for the family business. Most likely neither of us could have spelled or even defined *sophisticated* at the time. We were isolated farm boys, mostly unaware of life beyond our acreage.

We once delivered turkeys to a banker in Texarkana, Arkansas, who was raising prize turkeys as a hobby.

"Where you boys headin' when you leave here?" he asked.

We told him of a whim that hit us on the way there to swing by and see our Uncle Howard in El Paso on the way home. Since El Paso was somewhat south and west of where we were, we were obviously clueless about geography in general, let alone about the size of the state of Texas. The guy was amazed by our naïveté and informed us that we were much closer to home than El Paso. We decided to just go on back home.

By the time we went to college (Roger was two years ahead of me) the plane had become such an ordinary part of our lives we just took it with us and kept it at school in Columbia, Missouri. On breaks we flew it home.

Of course, when needed, we had it to make turkey runs. Roger ultimately went on to get his IFR (Instrument Flight Rules) license and flew planes and helicopters in the Army. I was content to stay with my VFR license. However, my flying *legacy* was not as limited.

My son, Scott, grew up flying here and there with me, but he never showed the slightest interest in flight. In 1990, while he attended college at UMSL, I purchased the rights to RE/MAX in Alabama, Louisiana, and Mississippi. Betty and I lived in Brandon, Mississippi, and had offices all over those states. One day, Scott called me.

"Hey, Dad, I'm here at school and was just sitting at my desk studying when something came to me out of the blue," he said. "I have three requests."

One was that I take him seriously concerning his desire to be a professional pilot; two, that I give my blessing on his dropping out of school; and three, that I help him with the $20,000 he needed for flight training.

He got all three wishes and eventually became the RE/MAX-Dixie company pilot. Our plane was a very fast, retractable-gear, single-engine Mooney. For Scott, it was just the beginning of a great career flying aircraft that would only get faster. When we sold 25 percent of our company in 1993 and moved back to Missouri, Scott became the pilot for the man who bought it. Before long he became the private pilot for Ted Turner and Jane Fonda and flew them all over the country. He currently flies one of the world's fastest jets for a company owned by Warren Buffet.

Over the years I have owned a Taylor Craft; two different Gruman Tigers; a Stinson; an Aronica Champ; a Cessna 120, 140, and 205 (the largest: six-passenger); a Mooney; and a Beechcraft Sundowner. I sold my last plane, the Beechcraft, in 2005.

From fifteen to seventy-two years of age, I have appreciated a lifetime of flight. But the planes I have owned and the experiences I have enjoyed are just the seeds of legacy. I am far prouder of Scott's piloting than my own, not just because the planes he flies are state of the art, but also because he has taken to flying as a true professional.

It is the same with my business and life experiences—legacy is *soaring* in the next generation and beyond. I relish the opportunity to have an ongoing impact, to serve others, to touch lives, and to impart the benefits of accumulated wisdom and experience to those who will best be helped by them along their journeys. We granted Scott's three requests because in them, I recognized my son taking hold of his destiny.

Destiny and flight are as synonyms in the thesaurus of my mind. Whether as a pilot or a passenger, the word I most connect to flying is "destination." The place and time of departure are also important, but the destination is what really has our attention.

A walk down to the corner store is simply, "I'll be back in a few minutes." A drive across state in the car is about "going out of town" or "taking a short trip." Cruises and train travel are about the experience of the ships and the trains. But flight is about destination.

Just seeing a plane overhead from the backyard inspires me to muse about *where*. Flying implies the great beyond. Like "genius" and "labor of love," in my life flying and destiny share a common reality in legacy.

Flying is not just getting off the ground, traveling by air, or getting someplace faster. It is a conquest of boundaries, such as gravity, pavement, road signs, speed limits, mountains, lakes, and oceans. It is freedom from crowds and traffic, a sense of controlled disconnection, high above the earth between one place and another, but otherwise part of no particular location.

Have you ever wondered what it was like for the astronauts who flew in the robotic chair, untethered, floating several hundred yards from the nearest humans, their space shuttle home appearing the size of a bug, earth glowing like a lighted globe in the distance?

Flying a plane has always been something like that for me.

More than anything else, I associate flying with perspective and vision. As elevation increases, so do horizons in every direction.

This principle has become inseparable from my consciousness, proven time and again as key to my quality of life, to business and relationships, to goals and dreams. If you want to expand your horizons, you learn how to soar . . . higher and higher.

When we look back, it is interesting to identify little things that impact the course of our lives. In 1948, Dad and I were driving turkeys to a farmer in Winner, South Dakota. Supposedly, we just had a few hours to go. But it was dark, right around midnight, when we encountered what we saw as a fork in the road not mentioned in our directions.

We went left. Somehow we found our way but did not arrive at our customer's residence until around daybreak. After we completed the delivery, we learned that the way we chose was much longer than if we had stayed to the right. So we headed back the other way.

As we neared the fork, we noticed that the road and everything along it was badly torn up. We found out that a tornado had ripped through there just after midnight—its path was along the section of road we would have traveled. What a difference a simple decision at that very time made—and what different results would have happened with another decision! It was after that trip Dad declared the time had come to travel and deliver turkeys by wings instead of wheels.

As I sat with Betty in a wide-body Jumbo Jet aimed toward Europe, I reflected that over the next three weeks I would meet with international business executives and give eight talks on Designing the Exceptional Life. The eagle associations and soaring motif that so naturally had become part of my professional signature were once again reality *and* symbol of core beliefs I looked forward to sharing with others.

From turkeys to soaring eagles . . . it seemed fitting that this journey started with turkeys. Turkeys seemed about as likely to soar as a farm boy from "nowhereville" northern Missouri. My own life had made me a believer.

Two roads diverged in a yellow wood,
And sorry I could not travel both
And be one traveler, long I stood
And looked down one as far as I could
To where it bent in the undergrowth;

Then took the other, as just as fair,
And having perhaps the better claim
Because it was grassy and wanted wear,
Though as for that the passing there
Had worn them really about the same,

And both that morning equally lay
In leaves no step had trodden black.
Oh, I kept the first for another day!
Yet knowing how way leads on to way
I doubted if I should ever come back.

I shall be telling this with a sigh
Somewhere ages and ages hence:
Two roads diverged in a wood, and I,
I took the one less traveled by,
And that has made all the difference.

—Robert Frost, *The Road Not Taken*

CHAPTER 2

DISCIPLINE = *OIMF!*

6:00 AM, DAY ONE

Important things stand out when they are absent. I was ready to go for my normal morning run and looking forward to it. But the routine was so set I could hardly get myself to open the front door because it just seemed like something important was missing. Out of another kind of habit, I patted my pockets as if checking for something.

After a look around, I glanced back toward the kitchen. I knew what it was. It just felt like there must be more that was missing.

No, I assured myself, *the protein shake . . . that's all.*

When I'm back home, every morning a personal-recipe protein shake supplies my fuel for running. But away from my own kitchen I had no fuel. Finally accepting this was the cause for my unsettled feeling, I opened the door, stepped outside, and walked toward the street.

While we were in England, we stayed in Virginia Water, a suburb of London, with Betty's daughter and son-in-law, Nina and Eric Zinn, and their two children, Sarah and Jason. The Zinns had moved to the UK three months earlier because of a promotion Eric received within Eli Lilly. At the end of the short driveway I turned and admired the Zinns' house. It was red brick with dark timber accents and striking red tile facades on its three prominent peaks. The English Tudor appearance suggested a much earlier era than its actual 1990s construction. English homes have names. This one was named Lanscomb House.

In this affluent area, "cottages" of earlier make were routinely torn down and replaced with modern estates. Lanscomb House was one of the modern estates, but with a throwback English charm. I turned and began to jog.

Lanscomb House is on a road called Nun's Walk, which feels more like a path through Sherwood Forest, a tunnel of tall conifers on the way to Rivendell, or a quiet corridor deep in the Hundred Acre Wood. It connects to Abbey Road (not *the* Abbey Road) and that to Christ Church Road. Virginia Water is in Surrey County, where many small towns—one to two thousand residents each—are strung together by two-lane "High" streets (like "Main" streets in rural America). Each town's High Street contains a diversity of stores in just a few rows in a central location. They cover all the basics for daily needs, making the towns independent.

Christ Church Road is Virginia Water's High Street. Of course, every village also has pubs along High Street. Virginia Water has two: the Wheatsheaf and the Rose and Crown, which boasts an original building over four hundred years old.

Houses are plentiful, though mostly unseen, throughout the thickly wooded suburban village. Tall walls of shrubs hide them from the street. The sense of order is profound. You can tell the architecturally arranged and sculpted bushes, fences, walls, hedges, and trees have received meticulous tending.

As I ran, the strong impression of decorum enlarged my already supreme appreciation of discipline. It was obvious in the mastery of botanical arts, architecture, engineering, masonry, and many other represented skills. But less obvious were the disciplines in the fields and livelihoods of musicianship, finance, athleticism, leadership, science, academia, and government that enabled people to live in such luxury. The area is home to Prince Edward, golfer Ernie Els, legendary rocker Phil Collins, and a number of other English celebrities, lords, ladies, and dukes.

I couldn't help but think of our son-in-law, Eric, and his new position: financial director of Eli Lilly, UK and Northern Europe. Because he practiced discipline in academic study, professional focus, and faithful organizational service over many years, he and his family have the opportunity to live in this exceptional community.

That jog in Virginia Water was a rather auspicious beginning to my three weeks in Europe. One of the most notable documents in all of history, the Magna Carta, was signed just minutes from the Zinns' home. In the heart of Virginia Water is the fabled Wentworth Club, headquarters of the PGA European Tour.

Since I am not a dedicated golfer, my morning run would not be in that direction. Leaving the neighborhood, I went instead through Virginia Water Park, a "Mecca" for walkers, runners, cyclists, and dog lovers. The park and the shores of nearby Virginia Water Lake—used for scenes in the Harry Potter movies—lie within the Windsor Great Park system, which contains fourteen thousand historic acres of scenic paths, large English gardens, waterways, and polo fields.

Somewhere amid the vast acreage, I was told, is Hampton Court Palace, former home of King Henry VIII. Ascot Racecourse, also within a short jog's distance, is closely associated with the Royal Family and hosts the annual Gold Cup and prestigious King George VI and Queen Elizabeth Stakes.

These merge into the Royal Landscape of Windsor Castle, not far from my unusually light steps and quick pace. The home of the queen is the largest inhabited castle in the world, with parts of it more than nine hundred years old.

I needed a few morning jogs to process the fact that all this was simply a morning's run from the home in which we were staying.

I like to name things. My weekly informative email, the *Eaglezine*, goes to more than 15,000 readers every Friday morning with a title highlighting the unique theme of that issue. For example: an issue released after Betty and I are blessed with a new grandchild might be titled *Tom Hill's Patriarchal Eaglezine!*

Regarding running, I had already experienced the Amazing Run, the Awe Inspiring Run, the Wish I Wouldn't Have Eaten That Before I Ran Run, the High Altitude Run (many of those), the *Too* High an Altitude! Run and many, many others. But I could not recall a WOW! Run in my past. I decided this was the Wow! Run.

Betty is not an early riser. She has occasionally explained that if God wanted her to see the sunrise He would've made it happen at noon. So every morning at a comfortable hour I fix her a cup of coffee and deliver it with an "I love you."

On days when I have to leave early for meetings, I prepare the coffee maker for her to simply press a button, and I leave the "I love you" note attached to her mug.

However, while staying in the Zinns' home in Virginia Water, I didn't have the privilege of serving her coffee. Nina enjoyed the opportunity to wait on and pamper her mom for a few weeks.

Back at the house after the Wow! Run, I showered and read. Reading is one of the most critical disciplines to my professional acumen and ongoing personal development, so I knock off about four hundred books each year. Just about the hour I realized it was time for Betty's coffee, Nina was there delivering it.

It wasn't even midmorning and already two significant omissions from my daily routine had me feeling something like as if I were driving on a flat tire. The protein shake is a discipline of personal physiological benefit. But service and expression of love to Betty is a discipline more akin to breathing, with benefits intended for her reaching every part of my being—not to mention the contribution to our wealth in marriage. She is a treasure, a true gift from God. So gestures like the morning coffee are ways to tell Him thanks as I let her know how precious she is to me. I started thinking of a way to say "I love you" instead of the coffee service that day.

Such importance on aspects of a daily routine might appear rigid to some. After all, I devoted time to my morning run, prayers, and my usual amount of reading. Three out of five is on the up side. But here is my definition of discipline: *Doing things you know you should do until they become a habit.*

Genuine habits are not disrupted without bother. These habits in particular are born of two pillars of conviction. One conviction is that we all have a moral obligation to be the very best person we can be. Thus, the protein shake is more than just healthy intake.

The second conviction is a moral obligation to positively impact every life I encounter. This begins at home with my wife. And since I love her, what could be more natural than finding ways to celebrate her with service?

Discipline is the key factor in what I call *OIMF!*—getting the *Odds In My Favor!* This, of course, does not guarantee I will have a thriving marriage because I fix my wife her coffee in the morning, perfect health because of daily protein shakes, or a home in Virginia Water because I habitually master the details that maximize my professional potential.

But disciplines like these are steps in the right direction, steps that collectively get the odds in my favor. They create positive attitude that spreads through all areas of my approach to daily activities and interactions—establishing victory momentum and cultivating anticipations of success.

Most importantly, these are factors anyone and everyone can manage and master.

There is no discipline gene. Some people actually believe there is. No, they wouldn't admit it, but you hear it in the way they talk: "Oh, he's one of those discipline types!"

Sorry, you can't get off that easy. *Doing things you know you should do until they become a habit* is not the proprietary right of an elite class. But it will put the odds in your favor for winding up in one. Now, that is some worthy *OIMF!*

The worst mistake—and unfortunately the most common—is the belief that discipline begins with pedigree or the inclination of a particular personality. The light didn't go on for me until I had crossed the half-century mark on my journey. I believe with all my heart if I can do it, anyone can! Trust me, I wasn't always a man of discipline and deeply ingrained principles.

When I was a kid growing up on a turkey farm in rural mid-America, life was pretty simple, though not necessarily easy. I was born in 1935, in our home twenty minutes from Kirksville, Missouri, and was my parents' second son. Another brother and a sister joined us later. Back then we had dirt roads, no electricity, no indoor plumbing, and no telephones—I believe the nearest phone was twenty miles away in Kirksville.

Daily life on a farm included abundant chores for a growing boy. In fact, in the summers it seemed there was *nothing but* chores to be done. We rose at 4:30 AM and worked until breakfast. After breakfast we returned to the farm and worked all day. Grade school interrupted the routine, but with one teacher and eight students in a one-room schoolhouse, this also seemed chore-related. My favorite part of the experience was riding my horse, Rainy Day, to school and back each day. That was my life until age fourteen, a solid introduction to high work ethic.

It was a twenty-mile bus ride to attend junior high school in Kirksville. I felt like an outsider because I *was* an outsider. Most of the other kids lived in town and had long-established friendships and cliques.

My parents were wonderful Christian people and provided a comfortable, secure home environment. But somehow that did not develop a high self-esteem in their diminutive second child. Small for my age, I saw my older brother as a combination stud/genius. He had already attended Kemper Military Academy, was quite a bit smarter than me, and made better grades. The concern, "I don't measure up," was constantly in my mind, leading me to believe I needed to please everyone to get them to like me.

FFA (Future Farmers of America) was a natural place for me to feel comfortable and perform well. In my sophomore year the FFA teacher, Oliver Barnard, took an interest in me. He visited our farm, encouraged my involvement in public speaking (making presentations before other classes), and helped me become a "Star Farmer." I remember feeling that he believed in me.

Those accomplishments gave me the confidence to run for the class presidency. Though I ended as runner-up, the experience was another boost to my esteem.

In 1951 I found out just how supportive my parents were. Only 127 kids were in my entire class, so the football coaches did not have the luxury of being picky. I tried out for the team and became a 135-pound offensive guard. Lining up against six-foot tall, 200-pound *real* football players was an eye-opener for me. But my parents didn't care that their son was not a headliner or future collegiate athlete. All that mattered was that their son wanted to play football.

Since the team practiced after school, I did not have a bus ride home. In order to make my football goals work, they rented a room for me at a boarding house near the high school. I lived there during the week, and then they brought me home on the weekends to be with the family.

This was a one-season foray into the gridiron trenches for me, but it demonstrated how far my parents would go to support my interests, however small my interests were.

It was around this time my brother, Roger, and I learned to fly and began making the turkey deliveries in Dad's Cessna.

Looking back, I see those as special times. But back then we only thought of it as what was necessary, and a sizable responsibility at that. We had a list of fifty things to check thoroughly before starting the engine. We didn't want our flying careers—or our lives—to end prematurely. So seeds of discipline orientation were sown early on in the seat of a Cessna 170 . . . and it just took several decades for them to germinate!

Appreciating the exotic side of flying a plane at such a young age might have benefitted me and at least stirred a sense of adventure and ambition. But I lacked the appreciation, so it did not have that effect. In fact, when I attended classes as a freshman on the campus of Missouri University I had zero aspirations.

My parents had very little college education, so it was a pretty big deal to be there. Still, I felt more overwhelmed than inspired. My inclination was not to be disciplined but to drift on whatever winds life served.

One of the prettier ones it blew in was Carol. I was nineteen when we met—no job, no money, and incomplete college education. She was also a nineteen-year-old freshman at nearby Columbia College.

If I were honest about the reason we got married, the answer would be, "Just because." Her parents were totally against it. They probably noticed I had the maturity of a five-year-old and the self-centered disposition of a boy nursing a poor self-esteem. Nevertheless, in 1955 Carol and I married. Carol dropped out of school and got a job so I could continue my education.

That plan worked until one October day in 1956 when I was sitting on the steps in front of a building on my university campus, and a perfect stranger sat down next to me.

"You look like a guy who would make a good teacher," he said. Then he offered me a job on the spot—a junior high and high school teaching position in Auxvasse, Missouri, a small town twenty-seven miles away.

When I explained I had no degree and no teaching experience, he promised a quick certification process.

Before I knew it, I was no longer *in* school but was *teaching* school for $300 a month. I was only a few years older than the seniors in my classes. For most of the school year I didn't even thaw until lunch, because this was mid-Missouri and my only transportation was a Harley-Davidson motorcycle.

Soon I was not only teaching junior high and high school classes but also coaching junior high and high school baseball, basketball, and track for the same $300 per month. The kids responded well to me, and their parents seemed to be thrilled with the impact I made. But the responsibilities took all of my time, keeping me from getting back to my own education. Once, when I talked of quitting, some parents scraped together $30 so I would stay—not $30 a month, just a one-time assistance of $30.

This should have been a wakeup call, a clear message identifying the rut I'd slipped into. But I did not get it.

During the summer I had a job with the University of Missouri *Labor Gang*. We cleaned, landscaped, picked up trash, moved chairs, rearranged furniture, and did whatever grunt work needed to be done. This was during the summer of 1957, and I was on a recreational league baseball team that had a game in Auxvasse, a half an hour away. My boss freed me to leave a half hour early to get to the game in time.

I was flying on my Harley 54, because I knew my time was limited and I still had to change into baseball pants. On Ashland Road, all gravel, I was pouring it on down a hill. At the bottom was a 90-degree turn to the left that, if you hit it right, would slingshot you the fifty feet or so onto the one-lane metal bridge over Hinkson Creek. I had done this many times without incident—in fact, I don't remember ever seeing anyone approach the bridge from the other direction.

After hitting the turn just right, the "Hog" beneath me was growling for the bridge, which, to my utter shock, was occupied by a large, commercial plumbing truck.

I had nowhere to go. The truck was just over halfway across the bridge. And it left no room between its sides and the metal rails of the bridge.

I was going too fast to hit my brakes on the gravel, and the rocky creek bottom was twenty-five feet below the bridge on each side.

Choices!

Perhaps in that instant I decided I would rather be dead than maimed, who knows? But I aimed at the truck, held my breath, and closed my eyes, awaiting impact. When I opened them again I was on the other side of the bridge accelerating away from the back of the truck. I had no clue as to what had just happened.

Skeptics will say otherwise, but there's no doubt in my mind that some sort of divine intervention occurred on the Hinkson Creek Bridge that day.

That was the wakeup call I needed. After a two-year detour from college, my teaching stint was over. I went back to Missouri University that fall to finish my bachelor's degree.

That same year Carol and I had our first child, Marie. Our second, Terri, arrived in 1958; our third, Michelle, in 1965; and our fourth, Scott, in 1969. After completing the bachelor's program, I got my master's.

By 1971 I was superintendent of schools in Green City, Missouri, and was offered a full scholarship at MU for my doctorate work. Along with climbing the academic ladder, I was experiencing tremendous personal growth. As I did, Carol withdrew. By 1972 our marriage was unraveling and would continue to do so over the next four years.

The biggest problem with our marriage was the fact that I was totally focused on my career—myself. I was not the least bit interested in investing any focus on our relationship, on Carol.

In the spring of 1976 I moved out. We went to counseling for a while but made no progress and finally decided to divorce. It was an amicable process. We used the same lawyer and had no tension whatsoever over *things*.

Still, it took its toll. I was an emotional wreck.

Shortly after the divorce I received a promotion at the university and moved to Cape Girardeau to be the Southeast Missouri Regional Director for University of Missouri Extension Service. I was responsible for the educational budget over seven counties. Yet, with my marriage of twenty-one years trashed and my children two hundred miles away, this was the lowest point of my life.

Between 1972 and 1976 John Denver's music was extremely important to me. It never was before and has not been since, though I do still appreciate it. Something about his sound and lyrics during that period deeply resonated with me. I later discovered John and I had a kindred spirit beyond just the lyrical—John was also a light aircraft pilot.

I try to attend a major aircraft show in Oshkosh, Wisconsin, every year. In 1993 I flew there in my 182 Cessna. While talking with someone about some new experimental aircraft I heard an unmistakable voice behind me. I turned around to see John Denver standing just a few feet away.

We had a nice talk, mainly about airplanes. But I was also able to tell him what an impact his music had upon my life. We don't always get those opportunities. But when we do it is critical to take them.

Of course, all of us want to be the one to make the big contributions in others' lives, while not being particularly interested in needing others' contributions in our own lives. When life helps us get over ourselves, we discover the need is mutual and relish the chance to tell others of their importance. Those chances are more limited than we know.

Our life is a faint tracing on the surface of mystery,
like the idle, curved tunnels of leaf miners
on the surface of a leaf.
We must somehow take a wider view,
look at the whole landscape,
really see it, and describe what's going on here.
Then we can at least wail the right question
into the swaddling band of darkness,
or, if it comes to that,
choir the proper praise.

—Annie Dillard

CHAPTER 3

THE UNLIKELY

9:00 AM, Day Two

London! Vast, sprawling, dense, colorful, busy, thriving London! Six hundred (plus) miles of urban wild, over eight million people ... *overwhelming* would not be an overstatement.

London is the Royal City, less than a century removed from ruling a quarter of the earth's population. There is a crossroads-of-the-world spirit of ambition that dazzles at a glance, a regal quality to its architectural dressings, and a sense of history on every peak, every façade, every bridge, every nook and cranny. Its equilibrium is a tension between venture and expedience. Optimism is its golden rule.

With some time before a lunch meeting with the Vistage group at Red Hill, my first presentation, I decided to fit in a little sightseeing. Betty stayed at the house. Her priority was to focus on her time with Nina. For her, all sightseeing would accommodate the mother-daughter schedule. London would have to wait.

I took the Virginia Water train in to London, a forty-minute ride, and got off at Waterloo Station on the banks of the River Thames. The Eye of London, a massive modern Ferris wheel designed as a symbol of the new millennium, is there towering over London. Big Ben is there. The Westminster Bridge is there. And most important, a taxi was there, sitting outside Waterloo Station as if waiting just for me.

My taxi ride was like a trip through a "Disneyland" of typography. Stylish lettering seemed to adorn every passing address as my driver demonstrated mastery of angle and swoop to avoid stopping. Whether bold or elegant, etched on glass, or gilded onto iron, neon script hanging in a window, or the hand painted Old-World-English of a pub sign projecting from a brick wall and hovering above the sidewalk, identities interacted in a cultural currency of ABCs.

There is a square mile of pure labor force in east London—I am told no one actually lives there. During the day over five hundred thousand people set "The City" abuzz with employment activity. Two thousand years ago it was Roman Londinium.

You learn all kinds of things like this when you actually visit a place and speak with its residents. I thought, for example, that Big Ben was a clock or a clock tower. But, according to a little verse I ran across on location, it's actually a bell.

Not the clock, not the tower, but the

Bell that tolls the hour.

I started out as an educator, a calling that continues to motivate me. Like all prepared educators, being educated is a constant passion for me. Aside from reading, meeting people, asking questions, and poking around where curiosity leads and epiphany await is the best way to learn—the most fun, for sure. More than a sightseer, I was a story chaser. With its history and diversity, London is a city of abundant fascinations. Stories are behind every cornerstone, on and in every corner.

Framed by hanging gardens above and potted gardens below, windows are the auctioneers on the streets, the look, the display, and reflection—the beckon and the echo of London trade.

But they have competition. In some areas street traders—migratory merchants surrounded waste-deep by boxes of livelihood—zipped by in twos and threes with every passing neighborhood. In others, giant sky-reaching structural marvels of stone, marble, glass, and chrome lingered despite my driver's lead foot. I was mesmerized by the blurry amalgam of wood, stucco, terra-cotta, colored ceramic tile, polished brass, textiles, stone, brick, steel, concrete, bronze, and the ever-present glassiness of the millennial metropolis. Tucked between all, the religions of the world were represented in houses of worship of every national and ethnic motif.

Perhaps because of the commonness of gray and rain and fog, even in the daylight hours the lights of London are prominent. Tall, black, wrought iron streetlamps are what we imagine from Dickens novels. Colorful modern 3-D lighted signs—some the size of the red double-decker buses, some much larger—broadcast the international iconography of capitalism. Ubiquitous strobes and lanterns illuminate walkways, bridges, statues, water fountains, and waterways. London is a city of lights.

And time! It's not just Big Ben's clock, Londoners do like to know what time it is. The city's architects oblige the obsession.

Have you ever been traveling and wanted to get on your knees in the seat, press nose and fingers to the glass, and just stare, enthralled? It wasn't easy, but I resisted.

12:45 Red Hill Place, Surrey County, London, Day One, Presentation One

Everyone was well dressed. But I knew there were many stories for every person seated before me, stories not represented in the professional appearance.

We enjoyed an exquisite lunch while I casually glanced around and acquainted myself with my audience. Acquaintance, however light, inspires a different approach to every conversation we have, whether one-on-one or with a large group. Sometimes that approach takes the form of an observation, sometimes humor, and sometimes a question . . .

Why do some people "*get it*" and others don't? This fascinates me as much as anything in the whole wide world of experiences in which I so ardently involve myself every day. Same parents, same home, same neighborhood . . . not precisely, but, *mostly* the same advantages and disadvantages . . . yet, one thrives and another flounders. Sometimes one thrives and three flounder . . . five . . . ten. You know what I mean—you've seen it. Fascinating, don't you think?

It was as if the entire group of people nodding their heads were answering aloud in unison, "Yeah, it really is. Please explain it; we've always wondered about it too."

I laughed.

I don't have any answer for it. It just fascinates me.

We all laughed. I allowed a little time for us to enjoy each other, to look around. I love these kinds of moments, like points of connection. Laughter has that magic. Looking over the group of eighteen business owners and CEOs, I continued.

But I do have some thoughts on attitudes and practices held in common by those who succeed and live exceptional lives . . . and on how nearly everyone—regardless of the past, regardless of unlikelihood as candidate for exceptionality, regardless of starting point—can own those attitudes, apply those practices, and thrive. Don't miss the subtlety in that. I mean, "regardless of starting point" . . . *your* starting point, where *you* are today, whatever success *you* have already known and presently enjoy. What next? That's the question we all care about, isn't it? What next?

I never take anyone's success for granted. It is hard earned. So every individual in the audience had this in common. I was proud of them. I was also one of them. I saw eyes express eagerness for challenges, revelation, and encouragement equal to my preparedness for their delivery. They were the eyes of people reaching, working, and striving to make a difference. They were eyes not so different from those of successful predecessors who bore tools of advantage as well as the burdens and tags of the unlikely on their way to historical impact. A palpable tension filled the room. I didn't expect that. Looking around, I sensed an unusual percentage of people present who expected to change the world.

JACKSON, MISSOURI, NOVEMBER 21, 1976, 7:00 AM

I had a great job. It was the reason for my transplant to southeast Missouri five months earlier. But I was living out of a small trailer ten minutes west of Cape Girardeau in Jackson, Missouri, and was flat broke at the end of each month.

I had pulled the trailer from Columbia to Jackson on July 1 with my ten-year-old Chrysler, which vapor-locked along the way, forcing me to pull onto the shoulder, turn the vehicle off, and wait for it to cool down. (You don't really want to be waiting around anywhere when your mind is full of guilt from a recent divorce, brooding about overwhelming alimony and child support payments, and heaviness from being disconnected from four children living two hundred miles away.) Like an old Missouri mule, when it was good and ready the car did deliver the trailer and me to our new address.

Many unmemorable days followed. They were bleak days that blurred together.

But on one cold November day, I rose early and turned on the radio. For some reason it was tuned to an AM station, which was odd. I was an FM guy from way back—I never listened to AM radio. Nevertheless, a speaker announced his name and informed listeners, "This is Layman Sunday at our church." Then he began to preach.

By the time he was done, I was a mess. Well . . . emotionally I was a mess. Spiritually I was the cleanest I had ever been. The guilt was gone, the brooding was gone, and the burdens were gone. Nothing circumstantially had changed, yet everything had changed.

I don't recall a word of the message, but I had cried hard. Down on my knees I had prayed hard . . . went on for an hour at least, just crying out to God, overwhelmed with repentance. When I got up, I knew I was completely cleansed.

As the layman preacher signed off I wrote down his name, the name and address of his church, and the call letters of the radio station. I quickly got dressed. I just had to go meet this guy. I had to tell him what happened, the impact he had on my life. After driving across town, I finally located the church at the address he'd given on the broadcast.

The pastor met me at the door. No one else was there yet. I explained the reason for my visit and told him the details—the name of the lay member of his congregation, the radio station, and time of the broadcast.

"Sir, we have no radio broadcast, never have. And we have no member by the name you've given me at this church. We're a small congregation, so, trust me, I know . . . no broadcast, and no one by that name."

Knowing the layman did not exist, I walked away with a profound assurance: *Everything's going to be OK.* From that point forward my life took on new meaning. Things began to fall into place. I was able to sell my trailer and get a house. I even got a new car—one that did not vapor-lock! The Holy Spirit of God had spoken to me that day in my trailer . . . on AM radio, no less!

I don't know what about the Red Hill crowd inspired me to tell them my story about the lay preacher on the radio. I don't talk about it too often, and then usually one on one. But when a large man strode toward me after my closing comments to the presentation, I knew what he wanted to talk about. My hand seemed like a ball inside a catcher's mitt as he shook it lingeringly, his other hand on my shoulder.

"Thank you for telling your story," he said, glassy-eyed.

"Which one," I asked for levity's sake.

"The one about the radio . . . your encounter with God. I have one much like it."

"For a long time I wouldn't tell anyone," I informed him candidly. "I thought no one would believe me—they'd think I just made it up or embellished or dramatized it for effect. I thought maybe it would make me look a bit flaky. I still don't tell it much, but when I do, I can be sure someone will come to me and confide something similar."

"I have never told anyone," he said. "The same issue . . . who will believe me? Same results too—it changed everything."

"Do you trust me enough to tell me?" I asked.

He thought for a minute, ran a hand through his hair, adjusted his glasses, put his hands in his pockets, and began his story. It was a doozy! He was just finishing it when we realized a line had formed behind him—and many people had heard it. There is nothing like a good story to make five minutes seem like one!

Back in the Middle Ages, 1155, Henry II issued a Royal Charter to the Weaver's Company. It denoted that the well-known establishment had earned the distinguished patronage of the Royal Household. This was the equivalent of knighting to those of trade and service.

Before long English merchants of every stripe fixed their eyes on this Royal prize. A tradition was born. Evolving into presentation of Royal Coats of Arms, by the eighteenth century, an annual calendar officially acknowledged all individuals and businesses holding Royal Warrants.

Not just anyone in the Royal Family can issue Royal Warrants, mind you. In fact, only four can do so: Her Majesty the Queen, the Duke of Edinburgh, the Queen Mother, and the Prince of Wales. Each can grant only one per establishment. Such establishments are easily identified on the streets of London by the Royal Coats of Arms mounted in their windows. Today, roughly nine hundred windows bear the exclusive designation, and even fewer can proudly display multiple warrants.

One of those is John Lobb, Bootmaker. The store has represented high-class and elegance for more than one hundred fifty years, and this artisan shop has dressed the feet of the rich and famous.

At the onset of the Edwardian era (high tide of English opulence) Prince Edward of Wales himself discovered the genius of John Lobb. From then on, those with the most discrete standards—and the finances to indulge them—have come to Lobb for custom-fitted footwear of the finest quality in the world.

Born in December of 1829, the founder, John Lobb, was a lame farm boy from Fowey, Cornwall, the son of John and Elizabeth Lobb. After developing his skills in the art of bespoke (made to individual order) shoemaking, the young Lobb headed to Australia and made a name for himself among the gold rush miners. He returned to London in 1866 and established the company.

One might think it a tall order for a rural-bred lad to set out on his own, master a fancy craft, and succeed in London by way of Australia. And taller still, for a company to survive the great depression and numerous deep recessions selling shoes that require the expert handling of professionals in more than a dozen specific disciplines—shoes that take better than fifty hours to create. Throw in two World Wars and the utter destruction of the building housing the company via the bombs of German blitzkrieg, and the ongoing Lobb legacy, its expansion to Paris and the display of multiple Royal Warrants above its front door is rather impressive.

What are the odds? What gets in the head of a small-town farmer's kid, lame at that, to take up shoemaking with such zeal that he should ultimately help others throughout the world walk with Royal style and comfort—along the way accumulating awards at international exhibitions and raising the already high standards in custom shoe-crafting?

Someone else with his beginnings might easily have been resentful about the many people around him who were *not* lame, preferring not to think about their advantages at all.

And what gets in the head of a turkey farmer's kid from rural Missouri to believe he can build a significant real estate business requiring many skills he had never implemented before—and do it so well he would get to become a success coach to prominent professionals? What makes a person believe a thriving marriage is possible when a previous attempt has failed? What makes any person see *possibility*, however unlikely, and seize it?

Of course, cynical opinions about the successful are common—a currency of flawed assumptions squeezed from mythic "sour grapes." Success by nature appears to possess advantage. The truth is, every person enjoying success, celebrating significance, and fashioning an exceptional life has gotten there by overcoming a measure of unlikelihood.

Examples abound:

Joseph, of the biblical account, started out favored by his wealthy father and later became powerful and wealthy himself, second only to Pharaoh in all of Egypt, the greatest nation on earth at the time and greatest imperial dynasty in history. But in between those favored times he had to survive the hateful envy of his ten older brothers, humiliating subjection to slave trade, false accusations, and a lengthy stint in prison.

Joan of Arc, a peasant girl born in eastern France, responded to a commission she believed came to her from God and joined the military during the latter days of the Hundred Years' War with England. Overcoming the defeatist attitudes of seasoned commanders, she rallied and led a resistance force that succeeded in lifting the siege at Orleans in little more than a week.

Her fame grew when she further led the French troops to victory in several significant battles, advancing her people toward liberation from English domain. Over the course of history, since her death at nineteen years of age in 1431, she has been one of the most celebrated of all historical figures by authors, artists, and theatrical producers, including Shakespeare, Tchaikovsky, and Mark Twain. She accomplished more—knew more success—in her brief nineteen years than most people do in ninety. Oh . . . and she had to disguise herself as a male to get into the army.

Abraham Lincoln was a brilliant and popular man. Even among the presidents of the most wealthy and powerful nation in history he remains exalted, honored for his leadership and political achievements. Yet, throughout his formative years he endured poverty and the oppressive ire of a father who appeared to despise him. Afterward, a long list of struggles, losses, and famously difficult battles with depression accompanied him on the road to his many accomplishments.

Margaret Thatcher was raised in moderate, comfortable economic circumstances that only improved throughout her life. Blessed with great intellect, as a young woman she received a degree in chemistry from Oxford University (having trained under Nobel Prize-wining scientist Dorothy Hodgkin). But she set her sights on politics, a road rarely visited by women in her generation. Abundant criticism and the vilifying print of the powerful opposition press seemed only to sharpen her convictions. Turning a string of early defeats and discouraging setbacks into political momentum, she became the first female prime minister of England and one of the most influential world leaders of the twentieth century.

Beethoven was a prodigy born into a deep heritage of musical excellence. When his Ninth Symphony premiered, he was in the fourth decade of public adoration that began when he was seven. At the end of the premiere conclusion, the audience exploded with thunderous applause. He had to be physically turned around to see the response. He was completely deaf.

If history tells us anything about the unlikely, it is that breath and courage to meet the present day is all the advantage a person needs to chip away at gloomy odds.

And we should not forget that the opposite is true. Advantage and opportunity can be squandered. Gossipers everywhere owe their most colorful and compelling material to "silver spoon" failures. Often, the trappings of "advantage" prove the greatest obstacle of all on the road to significance. The exceptional life is not just handed over by favorable circumstances.

The common eye
Sees only the outside of things
and judges by that,
But the seeing eye pierces
Through and reads the heart
And the soul, finding there
Capacities which the outside
Didn't indicate or promise,
And which the other kind
Couldn't detect

—Mark Twain
Personal Recollections of Joan of Arc

CHAPTER 4

AN ENGLISH
JOURNEY

1:00 PM, DAY THREE

I have always found the steely, clickity-clack percussion of a train on tracks to be romantic. As time and landscape pass by seemingly in equal proportions, the rhythm serves their flow into that realm of experiences *had*, while drawing nearer those just around the next bend or beyond the crest of a hill yet to be ascended. The romance and rhythm had inspired another movement—that of black ink on a page of the journal opened on my lap.

Or so I had thought.

Looking down, I discovered only one line, with no punctuation at the end.

That's funny, I mused, identifying the certainty of feeling I had been journaling. Evidently I had only gotten started when distracted by the sights out the window to my left, for how long I did not know.

My ancestors came to America from England, from this very area, in fact—the town of Shrewsbury in Shropshire County—not far from Wales in west-central England. My great, great, great . . . grandfather, William Hill, and his brother, Thomas, left from here and crossed "the pond" in 1652, eventually settling in what is now Virginia.

This is surely something genetic, I thought, analyzing a visceral and convincing sense of homecoming while traveling across their birthplace at one hundred miles per hour some three hundred sixty years later.

I traveled this "pilgrimage" phase of the five-country speaking tour alone, while Betty stayed with Nina and the grandkids. But it seemed like she was there. As my left shoulder pressed against the side of the train just below a window, I thought about the woman who taught me to value and participate in such things as gazing out at beauty. Adventure and big-story living, my beloved companion and me—just the way it has been these thirty-one years. What could be better?

I looked down again at the one line in my journal:

Blessed beyond measure

Seeing it in my own handwriting seemed to confirm a great and marvelous disparity between *this* reality and what might have been.

How did I get here? was as a subliminal message rising from between the letters on the page like steam from a steeping cup of English tea. The unanswerable proportions of the question ironically produced an easy, instant answer: *God's Favor.*

I simply knew it was true, so I wrote it down. It was not my usual detailed journaling, but the two lines were there on the page, each weighty with testimonial stories and gratitude:

Blessed beyond measure

God's Favor

We were somewhere between London, England, and Crickhowell, Powys, in central Wales. Crickhowell was the Day Three site for the second of eight speeches on the tour—the first one behind me and "in the books," as they say. By all appearances, Red Hill in Surrey County went well, a great start. Powys was next, the second opportunity to share my life experiences, humor, wisdom, and principles of significance with a Vistage group.

Like the first, the audience would be comprised of high-profile professionals—CEOs, corporate board members, business owners, civic leaders—accustomed to hearing inspiring presentations from an elite class of international public speakers. The honor that such groups would invite me to cross the Atlantic just to speak to them was not lost on me. Yet, anxiety was not part of the experience. I do not relate to public speaking as performance, but as organized, calculated sharing in the midst of many relationships at once. Whether I take a stage before a capacity crowd of hundreds or engage a small group, I do so with serenity.

Perhaps this, too, inspired the "Blessed beyond measure" declaration in my journal, a signature refrain constantly welling in my heart and echoing in my mind. When I'm asked the usual "How are you?" it just naturally comes out: "Blessed beyond measure."

Blessed is a belief backed by abundant examples in all aspects of my daily experience. "Beyond measure" is genuine astonishment at its proportions.

When I'm given a chance to speak to a group, my content always springs from this same place. And I am comfortable enough in my own skin that I feel how I am received only matters to the end that the blessing is passed to others. Like the engine pulling the train car in which I sat, I always sense the propulsion of blessing moving my journey along.

But how did I get here?

The question returned with an added urgency. I looked back out the window. Actually, this very question, though asked by others, birthed my public speaking years ago. Wanting to understand and apply principles behind my personal success, individuals and organizations had requested my reflections on how it all happened. But this was different. Now *I* was asking. The title of the talk for the tour was "Designing the Exceptional Life." Fittingly, there I was, alone on a train in a foreign country, waxing sentimental about the privilege of a life well lived—my life!

When I was a teenager flying around in a plane with my brother, I just thought it was my job. Only later, looking back, did I see those as special times. As a young guy, married and in over my head with the responsibilities of teaching and coaching high schoolers, I thought of it as $300 a month—survival . . . and maybe not enough. Only later did

I look back and appreciate two years invested in young people's lives. As a college professor I thought of my position as comfortable and secure. Only later did I appreciate it as foundational to greater things.

But sitting there on that train heading for Wales I saw *special* in real time. I knew the current experience was something extraordinary. My present activities were part of the very thing I was touring the English Isles talking to other people about: the exceptional life! I found myself wanting to retrace the path, wanting to recall with some savory satisfaction the way it all happened.

I stared out at the rolling hills of Celtic song, scenic lands of bagpipe and fiddle; of poetry and prayer; of knight and shepherd; of castle and cottage, crown and kilt; of Shakespeare, Milton, Swift, and Wordsworth; of Turner's pastoral palette and the gilded brightness of royal pomp; of hanging cumulous melancholy and war's long shadows.

Dappled sunlight upon sheep-speckled fields, vast and organized by wandering white-stone lines did not disappoint the anticipations of this lover of classical styles. Nor did their introduction of an occasional castle . . . storybook!

The conductor sounded the whistle, and soon the open landscape turned into decorative Tudor timbering in a quaint village of thatched cottages. Towns like this were plentiful and seldom reflected their Celtic or Anglo-Saxon origins or regional character, though many retained the Roman organization of a bygone era.

This town had the touristy appeal of a bedroom community, which revealed that we were nearing our destination. My wish to stop to look around came and went as quickly as the cluster of buildings in the English countryside. We were on a schedule. *Perhaps one day a return . . .*

I was noting similarities between the commercial agriculture dominant upon the landscape of the UK we were passing through and rural areas where I had lived back home. It especially reminded me of a particular section of the I-70 corridor outside Columbia, Missouri, a memory long in my past. The gratitude-laden question resurfaced: *How did I get here?*

Suddenly, a vivid memory emerged. Six stone columns on a greenway were surrounded by red brick buildings in the Francis Quadrangle on the campus of the University of Missouri in Columbia. I was surprised to discover that imagining walking through the columns toward Jesse Hall was as convincing as the many times I had actually done so years earlier. I almost felt as if I had grown up on that campus. "Career," "security," "success," . . . even "identity" had been developed there during those first laps of my adult life.

The columns stood iconic, paying monumental homage to strength, antiquity, academia, and survival. The pillars had originally been mere decorations on the front of Academic Hall and were all that remained when the building was consumed by fire in 1892. Appearing as Greek or Roman ruins, they possessed a power of symbolic connection between the campus and those times—those foundations of modern Western civilization, with its zeal for progressive academia, constitutional government, applied sciences, sophisticated economic prowess, and cultural dynamism.

Maybe more than the agricultural similarities between regions stirred these memories. Maybe they were induced by the sense of awe traveling through a country deep with historical ties to the Romans and sprinkled with stone monuments to former times.

Mine, though not as colorful, were no less foundational. On that University of Missouri campus I had found my way and excelled as a young man, first as a student, then as a professor—and finally, in the prime of career and manhood, I enjoyed a prestigious position complete with absolute security!

The proportions of such a social position are obvious in association with such an institution. It was not difficult to recall the tangible ownership of security in all its facets, like being a strong branch on a mighty tree proven over time through all kinds of weather and by abundant fruitfulness.

I smiled. Was that really me walking away from such a promise? I could still hear the chorus of friends and colleagues: "Why would you do that?"

And the answer I would love to recall? "Because the only thing bolder than attaining it is the gumption to let it go, that's why!"

But I really was *not* that bold or foolhardy. No, it wasn't boldness, though that was the ultimate requirement for making the move. It was belief. I believed I had more to offer, far more to grow into. I came to believe that success was only a necessary forerunner of significance. Belief and passion for significance, those were the motivators.

But where did *that* come from?

Suddenly the six columns, the MU campus, and their memory attachments were gone. A glance over my shoulder for a final glimpse, as I had at the passing of the small village many miles behind us, left me consciously back in my seat aboard the present reality enjoying its triumph over what might have been. I turned instead to my right and again thought of Betty, as if she were sleeping peacefully against my shoulder.

There, I thought, *is at least part of the answer to where the belief and passion came from.*

Betty believed in me and saw what I had to offer when I didn't; and she kindled my passion for significance, fanning it into flame with her encouragement. Because of her I was traveling through foreign lands sharing my story, *our* story.

Hours earlier, Day Three had begun in the usual way—a five-mile run.

Well, kind of . . . the distance was the same, but the setting was once-in-a-lifetime. I'd again jogged through the lush green of Virginia Water Park, filtered by a soft morning fog. The beauty left me especially grateful for the daily discipline of running.

I say "especially" because gratefulness is a *usual* part of the discipline. Andrea Bocelli accompanies my charge into the new day with his rousing tenor version of "The Lord's Prayer" via my headphones, and prayers of gratefulness, forgiveness, and supplication are also elements of my usual start of a day. The scenery took my gratitude to another level.

Of course, how well a day starts sets up everything else to follow. But the reverse is also true: how well the gift of a day is celebrated serves as motivation for starting the next day with lofty expectations.

This mentality continuously refreshes the language of "Soaring." Keeping a current accounting of gratefulness and celebration is intrinsic to the Eagle motif associated with my professional coaching business. It is a way of life. And as soaring goes, just breathing English air enhanced the beginning of days one, two, and three of the tour.

I looked out the window at a vastly green but otherwise rapidly changing landscape. An assumption we had crossed the border into Wales was supported by nothing evident. I hoped no one was looking, because I was smiling—one of those ear-to-ear smiles—just sitting alone smiling and shaking my head. A Hill in Hill-country. It was one of those rare experiences that eclipse high expectations.

Putting pen to page, I was determined to get some fresh reflections into my journal. It is important to me to keep accounts of presentations and the people I meet along the way. But the writing was not at all like my normal journaling. Distracted and patchy, it was comparable to a random sampling of sound bites, a bunch of notes on the presentation the previous day in the Surrey County suburbs of London.

I recorded something of relief that the tour had gotten off to a good start, putting to rest concerns about connecting well with people of different communication sensibilities, as the English surely are. I know from experience such things can be interesting at times. I noted that the Vistage chair, possessor of a higher professional pedigree and superior résumé, had given me a rather flattering introduction.

Few things are as enjoyable or humbling as being lauded by someone you hold in high esteem. Still, my reaction to such introduction is always the same: a temptation to whisper to someone, "Who's he talking about? I thought *I* was the speaker today!"

Should I ever lose this kind of humility, I don't need to worry that I'll be too proud for long. My dear Betty is a truly faithful friend in many ways. Keeping counsel of my humility is one. Once I returned from giving a talk eager to tell her about the powerhouse of who's whos I had been given the opportunity to inspire.

"Do you know how many important people there were in that room?" I gushed.

"One less than *you* thought there were," she replied.

Lesson learned!

The Red Hill gathering, too, had consisted of professionally "important people." But it could have been an assembly of locals in an Elks hall or a crowd of young adults in a university auditorium. They would have been just as important and my primary message would have been the same. While people of varying geographic and socioeconomic backgrounds chase widely different goals, one universal passion pounds within every human heart: the desire for significance.

Given an opportunity to coach a group or individual on principles of success, I feel a sense of moral responsibility to communicate proven, practical strategies to establish and expand significance. It is one of the obvious answers to the question, "What am I here for?"

Traveling through Wales was a one-time opportunity. With little remaining to the train ride I gave up on journaling, closed the book, and put it away. The train whistle blew. Outside, pastures and commercial agriculture had given way to variegated gray-browns. The rugged remnants of a mining era of the past were dispersed between emerald slopes, peaks, and valleys for which the British Isles are famous.

I was eager for the next opportunity to meet people eager to pursue *their* upcoming opportunities. The pockmarked scenery with occasional signs of human residents held something unique and welcoming. The train whistle blew again, and I felt as if it were announcing my arrival. It wasn't arrogance or vanity, just a very high sense of purpose. For a messenger delivering instructions on soaring, the dynamic setting was a true inspiration.

He clasps the crag with crooked hands;
Close to the sun in lonely lands,
Ring'd with the azure world, he stands.

The wrinkled sea beneath him crawls;
He watches from his mountain walls,
And like a thunderbolt he falls.

—Alfred, Lord Tennyson, "The Eagle"

CHAPTER 5

HUGE "LITTLE THINGS"

5:00 PM, DAY THREE, WALES

My driver let me know we had entered the vast grounds of Gliffaes Country House Hotel. We traveled another half mile up a steep drive to the magnificent inn. It reminded me of massive Southern plantation homes from my years living in the land of Dixie. The hotel had been purchased some time ago and converted from a private estate.

The environment and everyone I encountered seemed to share a casual demeanor. *Betty would fit right in*, I thought. Inside, the hotel was stately and grand, quite ornate, yet it offered a comfortable, homey welcome.

The rooms were small for such a large building. After getting settled into mine I decided to walk around before dinner. I discovered a former stable adjacent to the hotel was the conference center where I would speak the next morning—the second day of the trip.

Walking to the other side of the hotel, I anticipated looking out over a glorious vista. I was not disappointed. Situated on top of a bluff at least three hundred feet tall, Gliffaes Country House Hotel was worth a visit just for the view. A small river cut the valley below. Cattle congregated along both banks and many others wandered throughout the rolling pastures of the reclaimed mining territory. Once again I thought of Betty, lamenting she wasn't there to share the experience.

January 15, 1979

I worked for the University of Missouri, but my office was on the campus of Southeast Missouri State University, where my daughter, Terri, attended college. Between classes, she paid me a surprise visit.

"I met the neatest person, Dad. Just something about her . . . I think we're gonna be best friends."

"That's nice, Honey," I answered, somewhat preoccupied. Terri had apparently met this person in their first class of the second semester, which had just started. But I wasn't really paying enough attention to get the details.

"Dad, I'll give you one guess what her name is."

I tried to mentally pry myself from my work, enough to be a good sport. It didn't work. "Oh, I don't know. I really don't have any guesses, Sweetheart."

"Terri! Her name's Terri too. Isn't that great?"

"Wonderful. It should be easy to remember."

Quickly the two Terris were indeed best friends and in March, my Terri was going to St. Louis for a few days to hang out with the other Terri and meet her mom. When she got back there was more "great news."

"Dad, I met Terri's mom and she's wonderful! And . . . Terri and I were thinking . . ."

For the first time since the whole Terri duo thing came up, my full attention was on the subject. I almost said, "No way!" before she could say another word. But I was too slow.

"We think we would make super sisters. And . . ."

"No way!"

"You're single, and . . ."

"No way! No way, Terri. Don't even go any further."

"We just want you to go on a blind date. One date, get out and have a little fun. What could that hurt?"

"A blind date two hours away? Uh-uh, no, not interested."

She gave me one of those really disgusted looks only teenage girls can make and turned to leave. "Her name is Betty Camp."

In May of that year my father's health was failing, so I took him and Mother to El Paso to visit family. Terri decided to come along. The entire way there and back she talked to me about Betty. Finally, I asked her to get me a photo of this Betty lady. Days passed before I was told she didn't have a photo.

Oh, great! I thought. Needless to say, my interest was not soaring.

A month later Terri announced an arrangement I was obligated to cooperate with: the two girls and Betty and I were going to a Cardinals baseball game on July first. Throughout the week before the big event I asked when the game was to start. I got no answer. Then, a day or so before the game, the other Terri revealed that she could not go. To avoid awkwardness, my Terri decided she wouldn't go either. Since the scheme avoided no awkwardness for me, I, too, backed out, requesting Betty's phone number so I could call her to apologize.

She surprised me. When I said, "Let's just take a rain-check," Betty asked if I like baseball. I said, "Well, yes, in fact, I'm a longtime Cardinals fan."

Betty suggested it might be fun, then, to just go to enjoy the game, since we were both fans. That told me a lot about her. Some guy just tried to weasel out of a date and she had the self-confidence to adjust the nature of the outing instead of being offended. I also could tell she wasn't particularly looking for anything to come from the activity. She would have been comfortable with my answer either way.

July 1, 1979 (three years from that very low day I sat on the side of the highway brooding, waiting for my vapor-locked car to cool down) I drove the two hours from Cape Girardeau to St. Louis and met Betty Camp.

We spent three hours together at Busch Memorial Stadium thoroughly enjoying a Cardinals game and each other's company and tacked on another one or two hours over coffee. We talked easily, about books we both liked, about our daughters, about our worlds.

Betty, as it turned out, was not any more interested in the dating service our Terris cooked up than I was. That is why there was no photo. As the secretary to the CEO of a large manufacturing company, she was doing fine on her own and was generally content.

In October I proposed. Explaining that it was too close to her divorce, she turned me down. I tried again around Christmas and she said, "Yes."

We married on May 10, 1980, in A.P. Chapel, part of the student union on the University of Missouri campus. Terri and Terri dating service, though not in business long, was quite successful—a 100 percent rating, in fact.

8:00 AM, DAY FOUR, EARLY SESSION OF PRESENTATION TWO, WALES

The Wales group was unusually small, just six members. Vistage groups vary greatly in size. However, except for this one, those on the tour schedule were all about the same, an intimate fifteen to eighteen members. Aside from the size of the group, all else was the usual. Attendees reflected the typical Vistage membership profile—owners of small- to medium-size businesses and CEOs.

Vistage was started in Milwaukee in the 1950s as a vehicle for international business owners and CEOs to meaningfully discuss common issues with similar professionals who are noncompetitors. The original name was TEC (The Executive Committee).

The model for Vistage groups came from the mastermind concept out of Napoleon Hill's book, *Think and Grow Rich*. It is the idea of mutually beneficial professional synergy resulting naturally when people gather to share creative thought, inspiring and influencing one another with practical solutions and help. Each local group has a chair who takes the lead. The value to each member comes from what occurs in the group at the local level.

In February of 2000 I did my first presentation to a Vistage group. It was a spousal retreat, a group from Cleveland, Ohio, meeting in Naples, Florida. Since then I have made over six hundred Vistage presentations in eight countries, have met thousands of entrepreneurs and CEOs, and have made just as many friends. As a speaker I am there to influence those in attendance. But the impact on my life has been tremendous—incalculable!

I had actually never seen a group as small as the one in Wales. Perhaps that very fact affected my thoughts, which were on little things . . . little things with huge impact. Even as we socialized over breakfast my mind assembled the ideas and memories coming to it into a relevant opening to the talk.

Though I had a set presentation for the tour, this was the kind of intuitive adjustment that makes every speaking experience unique. Every group deserves a talk that is thoroughly planned for effective coaching but also tailored just for them. After a few introductory comments the morning session started with a focus on the small.

> It really does not take a lot to impact someone's life, change its course, maybe even turn someone around . . . start a transformation. Who knows, with a little momentum, perhaps a full-blown revolution will develop.

> We usually think revolution requires something huge, like exposure to a movement, the influence of a mentor, earning a college degree. And those do have great impact. But in my life, five contributions that made huge impressions and had

lasting, profound impact were great treasures in very small packages . . . word packages.

The first was delivered in my youth. Throughout my elementary education I attended a one-room school. Once my teacher, Mrs. Ford, and I were at the school alone. She looked at me and said, "Tommy, you should become a doctor. You'd make a good doctor."

Before that I never envisioned much beyond riding my horse to school. Of course, the fact that I remember this says something about the impression the statement made. But I believe its impact on my life has been much greater than memory. I am, after all, Dr. Tom Hill . . . ignoring my mother's answer, "The kind you don't go to," to a friend's question, "Just what kind of doctor is your son, Tommy?"

The second came as I approached my own half-century mark. In December of 1979 I proposed to Betty and she said a monumentally powerful little word, "Yes." One beautiful little lady attracted to me for who I'd become changed my life forever.

The third contribution, incidental but momentous, occurred in 1984. After Betty and I married, a nice promotion at the university came along. I was head of the Missouri 4-H program—supervisor of over thirty 4-H agents and twenty thousand volunteers with an office staff of eight master's- and doctor-level professionals. It was also a great time of reconnection with my four kids who were in Columbia, Missouri.

One day an associate came through, a 4-H agent from Nevada, Missouri. He tossed a couple of cassette tapes onto my desk and said, "Tom, you might enjoy these."

I didn't think much of it, but later played one of the cassettes in my car on my way home from work. It was nothing fancy—just a man named Jim Rohn speaking about the principles of success.

While driving around in the car together over the next weeks and months Betty and I listened to those tapes so much we literally wore them into pieces. Two things resulted: one, we sat down together and established our new priorities and committed to live by them the rest of our lives; and two, we decided, "We're going to become wealthy!"

Of course, anyone familiar with Jim Rohn knows the implications of "wealthy" are far greater than monetary riches. With meaning encompassing relational health, physical health, spiritual health and, yes, financial health, it can be thought of as holistic wealth.

January 1, 1986—eighteen months later almost to the day—I received the fourth life-altering word package, this one in the form of a casual suggestion. Betty and I were returning from a vacation in Florida. One of Jim Rohn's well-known challenges began with the question, "How high should a tree grow?" and ended with the answer, "As tall as it can."

Betty said to me, "Tom, you haven't grown as tall as you can."

We decided to swing by and visit my old college roommate who was living in Georgia. Turned out, he owned RE/MAX of Georgia. We told him about the commitments we made, as a result of information on the Jim Rohn tapes. He said, "If you want to get rich, why don't you come down here to Georgia and sell RE/MAX franchises."

"That's about the dumbest thing I've ever heard!" I responded. "I have three kids in college and one in high school, a great job with exceptional benefits and security. I don't have a real estate license and I have never sold a thing in my life!"

Driving home, we were in north Georgia when I asked Betty what she thought of the idea. Before she could answer, I reit-

erated *my* thoughts. "Betty, it's crazy! Straight commission
... no salary, no benefits plan? We'd have to risk everything."

Impact statement five was coming, and I was not ready for it.
She looked at me and said in her famously casual manner, "I
believe in you. Let's go for it."

The only problem was that she believed in me before I
believed in myself. Yet, March 10, 1986, I was in Georgia
selling RE/MAX franchises and once again living out of a
trailer—we would not own a home again for four years. It
was the beginning of a great journey I would have missed
had it not been for Betty.

Five little word packages entered my ears and over the course
of decades conspired to change my mind, conquer my heart,
and transform my life:

> "Tommy, you should be a doctor."

> "Yes."

> "Tom, you might enjoy these ..."

> "Tom, you haven't grown as tall as you can."

> "I believe in you. Let's go for it."

Though just six were in attendance, the Wales group was a lively,
engaging bunch!

When I paused at the end of the intro, preparing to move into the actual
beginning of The Exceptional Life presentation, my break in thought
gave opportunity for someone to ask a question—highly unusual for a
Vistage talk. The question was about making oneself available for the
impact of small things amid many huge responsibilities. It turned out
to be an excellent bridge to the foundational structure of the talk—life
priorities: spiritual, physical, relational, emotional, professional, and
financial.

At the halfway mark I like to give everyone a five- to ten-minute break
to stretch the legs and freshen up. During the break a man came up

and told me he was confused because he was experiencing burnout right when he should be celebrating the high points of his professional and financial success. He had been quite thrown by my prioritization order of the six key life elements: (1) Spiritual, (2) Physical, (3) Relational, (4) Emotional, (5) Professional, and (6) Financial.

"I have had those almost exactly reversed," he said, admitting that a couple of them had not been priorities at all. Feeling paper thin in each aspect of his life that wasn't professional or financial, he committed to rearranging priorities. We discussed some manageable adjustments, and I recommended a reading list on the subject. Like the pilots who crash because they run out of gas, I'm always amazed at how many people proceed far into their lives without evaluating these key elements.

These interactions are the best part of being a traveling speaker. After all, we are just regular folks connecting. I know what others want because the exceptional life is also my devotion. It was especially meaningful that the prioritization of the six life elements—the list itself—made such an impression on someone so early in the tour, as it was central to the talk for which the entire tour was created.

"Tipping Points" was the topic planned for after the break. But, for the sake of continuity, I decided to get started with some more *small* talk.

"Fascinated." "Frustrated."

Which of these words characterizes you more often? It isn't hard to figure out. It's simple, in fact. Which one of these words is most inclined to leave your mouth?

Isn't it interesting the difference a simple vocabulary adjustment makes? Just thinking each word separately produces two distinctly different emotional reactions. What do you think the impact of saying them is? And what about saying one or the other habitually?

Some time ago I intentionally began using the word "fascinated" when I felt like saying something frustrated me. It was not a cheesy mind trick. I realized the frustrating quality of situations causing me to *feel* frustrated naturally include a legitimate—maybe even equal—fascination.

Why do things frustrate us, after all? Because we don't understand them, right? How fascinating! "How could that person possibly behave that way?" Or, "What on earth is the problem here? Why isn't my plan working?"

The basis of frustration is something we don't comprehend. How fascinating!

You know what . . . the world is quite a bit more fascinating and far less frustrating to me today due to that one little verbal habit adjustment.

The subject matter appeared to be right on the mark. Though only six sets of eyes looked at me, those eyes held an intensity of intrigue.

How about this one: "concerned" or "curious"? "I'm really concerned about . . ." or, "I'm really curious about . . ."

That one really hits me viscerally. Certainly there are times "concern" is what you want to convey. But most times, I think we could replace it with the word "curious" and find it better represents what we mean. And more important: who we are. I am a very curious person. I know you all are too. That's how you got to be serial entrepreneurs. You can't help it. I much prefer responding to the world with ongoing curiosity than the deep concern required once in awhile. One word impacts my disposition and accurately conveys who I am.

Let me tell you what a friend and mentor once explained that changed forever my attitude about the importance of little things:

"Imagine a humongous solid steel ball—as big as a two- or three-story house—on an extremely slight decline, too slight to notice. You start out pushing it by yourself, pushing with all you've got. Think of selling RE/MAX franchises like that."

Don Hackenberger owned RE/MAX of Florida and the Carolinas. In February 1986, I was with him in one of his North Carolina offices getting some coaching from this veteran.

"You sell one. The guy you sell it to comes over and helps you push the ball. An added benefit of the sale you did not expect, but still no noticeable impact. Then you sell another and another and another . . . you've got five or six people now helping you push that ball. Still nothing. All together you keep pushing. You sell another and add another helper. Somewhere along the line you reach a tipping point—something unperceivable—and, while you're all catching a breather, you notice the ball is moving ever so slightly on its own. Before long it's picking up momentum."

How shall we picture the kingdom of God,
or by what parable shall we present it?
It is like a mustard seed, which, when sown
upon the soil, though it is smaller than all
the seeds that are upon the soil,
yet when it is sown, it grows up and becomes
larger than all the garden plants
and forms larger branches; so that the birds
of the air can nest under its shade.

—Jesus of Nazareth (Mark 4:30-32)

CHAPTER 6

G-CURVES AND TIPPING POINTS

ONE OF MY FAVORITE TOPICS in every presentation, the one that elicits the most post-talk discussion, is "G-Curves and Tipping Points." Tipping points have become part of my personal philosophy on growth. They are typically not noticeable, like trying to pick out a single atom in a glass of water and say, "See, that's the one that makes the whole thing wet and thirst-quenching."

Tipping points have great significance, but they have their celebrated moment in the environment of accumulated decisions, acts, and accomplishments of equal or greater significance. "The straw that broke the camel's back" is a common saying that conveys the concept, albeit, an unfortunately negative one.

Tipping points are *breakthrough* moments in personal and/or professional growth. They often include a shift to an entirely different level of capacity of personal and financial influence.

Where true tipping points differ from the randomness of one atom in a glass of water and a strand of straw among jillions carried by a camel, or even Don Hackenberger's illustration of combined efforts of "helpers" pushing a large steel ball, is that the tipping point is a predictable by-product of intentionality and method.

We may not know exactly what the tipping point will turn out to be, but we know how to advance toward it (encouraging it, you might say). We know how to purposefully manage the factors contributing to it—the focal point of relationship investments. And we know generally when to expect it.

The steel ball analogy is most relevant in its depiction of a direct line between accumulated relational wealth and personal growth. Human beings are created for relationship; that is, relationship is inseparable from a sound definition of what it is to be human. So we know personal growth depends on relational growth.

Things like professional and financial growth naturally follow. Growth itself is accumulating. A tipping point is the site of critical mass resulting in a growth leap.

Tipping points happen right around the eighteen-month mark, often *to the day*. I call this a growth (or G) curve. Eighteen months is not a magical number, it is a managed destination. It is not scientifically proven (yet), but it is an observable phenomenon. I have seen it time and time again in my own personal and professional experience and in the experiences of the many people I coach and with whom I associate. Grasping the importance of the eighteen-month G-curve can be aided by thinking of it in the context of the words "cosmic," "nature," and "reality." It's not science, but it's not a stretch to make such contextual connections.

In fact, when I am asked about the origin of the G-curve I often attribute it to Gordon Moore, citing Moore's Law, first published in 1965.

Moore was cofounder of Intel Corporation, which produced the world's first microprocessor under his leadership. He was a leading innovator of semiconductor integrated circuit technology used to develop microprocessors. Moore's accomplishments helped revolutionize the field of information processing, and he received just about every coveted award in the field for his efforts.

Moore's Law originally predicted a doubling of capacity of integrated circuits every twenty-four months—later adjusted to eighteen months. It enabled the estimation of future progress in integrated circuitry. The law continues to surprise skeptics with its accuracy.

Moore's Law as applied to personal growth might be less scientific, but it is equally uncanny in predictability and trend observation. That should not be surprising. After all, Gordon Moore was first and foremost a chemist. Like the rest of our universe, the physical reality of human beings is essentially chemical in nature, and yes, circuitry.

Hearing, for example, is the ear's conversion of signals at a molecular level; movements of electrically charged particles—ions—generate electrical signals in the organ of corti in the inner ear, which the brain interprets with atomic exactness. We are chemical tapestry, firing synapses, neural pathways, translated electrical impulses and neuroplasticity—the brain's astonishing ability to make adjustments in its own functional and structural development in accordance with external (environment) and internal (thought) influences.

I started thinking: *If Moore's Law predicts an eighteen-month doubling of capacity in circuitry, why wouldn't it apply to people carrying around the most elegant and sophisticated circuitry on the planet?*

Thinking turned to observation, and, sure enough, I watched it happen over and over.

Though Moore's Law came to be associated with nearly everything that changed exponentially (i.e., progress in genetics), Gordon Moore never intended it to be applied so liberally. He certainly had no personal growth curves in mind when he worked out its mathematical calculations. But I figured if I'm going to adopt the idea behind Moore's Law, I should give him credit.

An interesting aside about Moore's Law is that many experts believe it is actually, in greater part, self-fulfilling prophecy. The fact that Moore put it out there (initially based on observation) and it proved accurate created a compelling phenomenon by which competing microprocessor developers worldwide saw it as a mark to shoot for. Assuming it would happen—that somehow the evolution of technology would once again double capacity by the eighteen-month marker—the race was on to be the first to get it there, or at least not to be left behind.

This participatory intuitive aspect of the law's successful reputation was even more intriguing and instructive as applied to goals, disciplines, and the pursuit of personal capacity breakthroughs. After naming such breakthroughs the G-curve, I have seen so many examples that, had I been any good at math, I would have logged my data and composed an equation demonstrating its soundness. Alas, math is not my thing.

But that does not prevent me from enjoying science and placing confidence in what I observe to be true. In physics, quanta manifest themselves in the statistical nature of the knowledge of reality as observed/measured at atomic and subatomic scales.

Though the subatomic universe is nothing like the universe we observe, we recognize that everything identifiable as our *experience*—the macro of our everyday lives—begins in the micro. Though our appreciable experience is made of a continuity of energy, we find that energy is not continuous, but comes in discrete, indivisible units.

A simplistic handle on quantum mechanics might be: the mathematically based description of particle and wave interactions of energy and matter. Most importantly we will notice the synonymous quality of "measure" and "observe," in a universal maxim of quantum mechanics: Nothing is real unless it can be measured/observed.

Similarly, by observing personal and professional growth, we can say that what we recognize as accomplishment, success, and breakthrough is built of proven, indissoluble units called *principles*. Goals are principle-populated determinations. An intention does not leave the realm of whim and enter the realm of goals unless it is given measurable proportions; and it does not become reality until measured to be so.

Thus, not only are G-curves manageable and tipping points predictable, but they are the result of measurable and controllable elements of success applied systematically.

This is extremely important in terms of two other factors present and influential at all times: belief and motivation.

If we admire principles, goals, measurability, methodology, control, and success from an abstract, feel-good distance, we will never own them in our core being, where belief is formed and motivation is fueled.

In other words, it is possible to intellectually embrace the *idea* of "success" and actually *believe* its necessary components are *unnecessary*. In this case, a person quickly discovers there is no practical difference between his or her lofty ideas of "success" and a secret belief it is unattainable.

We must first commit to principles, goals, and disciplines as laws of nature foundational to the reality of success. Then we will possess the belief and motivation to apply them.

Knowing what we believe is critical for separation from things we don't believe, and also those we *have* believed but hope to overcome. A good defining question: "Do I believe principles and disciplines applied to measurable goals can actually alter habits and change a person's life?"

Depending on the answer to that question, a second and even more pertinent question will be: "Do I believe *my* applying these *will* change *my* life?"

If you can stay disciplined and focused on your goals for eighteen months, one G-curve, I say you can experience major breakthroughs in your life.

You can accomplish more and go further if you commit to *written* goals and follow through on the steps to make them happen in the context of an eighteen-month G-curve, a three-year plan (two G-curves), and a six-year plan (four G-curves).

Higher levels of success are typically connected to goals that are significant, relevant, and difficult. And true goals always meet what I call the SMART criteria: Specific, Measurable, Action-oriented, Realistic, and Time-sensitive. Here are some basics to the G-curve concept:

1. Focus on specific written goals.

2. Allot time daily to achieve your goals.

3. Recognize when you need assistance to achieve your goals.

4. Recognize knowledge you will need to achieve your goals.

5. Recognize obstacles to your goal achievement.

6. List tasks you must accomplish to achieve your goals.

7. Organize tasks into a plan to achieve your goals.

It is ultimately about the accumulation of daily, seemingly "little" victories and accomplishments that culminate in a very small thing called a tipping point. But the result is a huge thing: a breakthrough in personal and professional capacity!

Immediately following one talk a man greeted me with the confession that he had felt there were too many pressing things on his mind for making room in his schedule to attend the presentation. One of the other members was responsible for persuading him to be there.

"I'm glad I came," he said.

I had noticed him either taking notes on the content of my speech, or making notes about something else *during* it. He appeared to be working out some math. Standing before a small group, such things tend to be conspicuous. When I asked what he had heard, he answered with cryptic English brevity, "Legacy growing pains—loud and clear."

"*Your* legacy, I'm assuming. Tell me one thing that made you recognize that," I pressed.

"Your assertions concerning the eighteen-month growth curve . . . 'Universal' is a bold claim. But I reviewed past achievements, the big ones, the ones that advanced my business to an entirely new category of scope and profitability. They all followed that pattern: breakthroughs, 'tipping points,' as you say . . . sure enough, always right around the eighteen-month mark."

"So, anything more you can share about your legacy or its growing pains?" I questioned, snooping a bit for an interesting revelation or two.

He shrugged. "Just a project I really believe in . . . *very* consuming and expensive, mind you. I met with my board of directors just yesterday on *Can it* or *Give it a few*. Usually they are the cut-right-to-it types. But they were split on this one, lots of careful words for my sake . . . milk-toast! I took it hard. But now I'm encouraged. They did not vote to *can it*, and we are just into month sixteen by my calculations." He produced a list of goals with the title atop the page: Next Two Months.

So, he was making notes, not taking notes, I thought, pleased that he got what he came for, even if he did not hear much else of the talk.

"One idea well executed can change your life forever," I encouraged, thinking he probably missed it in the presentation. But he surprised me by again holding up his piece of paper and pointing. There it was in large, aggressive writing between quotation marks, one of my strongest convictions. He looked at the paper and turned it over. Finding what he was looking for, he held it out and again pointed. "I like this one even better."

What gets measured—gets done!

"I've been far too 'shoot from the hip,' as you Americans would say. Served me well, thus far, but it's time to sharpen things a bit, I say."

The man was obviously successful. He also was ready to place a higher premium on fine-tuning and calculation. I told him about my leadership lesson manual and offered to send him one. "The focus is on learning the key principles, how to apply them on a daily basis, and staying disciplined for eighteen months in order to change habits—whether personal or organizational. The key is changed behavior patterns resulting in growth."

"I'll look forward to receiving it," he said, handing me a business card.

Like a moon
Reflecting the sun of my compulsive orbit,
Do I wobble and not spin,
Travel a capricious line,
Make tracks in the night sky
Like the arbitrary steps of some milling beast?

I am a man upon this earth,
Chemical poetry,
Intended and intentional,
Like a flash of lightning dancing
Across the horizon,
Briefly brilliant,
Abundant,
Eternally thankful.

—Russell Stuart Irwin
from *Dancing*

CHAPTER 7

LIGHTNING

12:20, JULY 15, 1992, MOUNT YALE, COLORADO

We had gotten onto the mountain late, a major violation of our commitment to one another as climbing partners. Yale is part of a series of "Fourteeners" west of Buena Vista, Colorado, called the Collegiate Peaks. There are numerous routes on these mountains. We decided on the shortest route—southeast, climbing northwest—which was the most difficult. I would like to say it was because of our careful planning and experience-informed judgment. But it was completely dictated by the lateness of our start time. By the time we set out, we had just about zero *OIMF!* factor on our side.

Our standard goal was to be up and back, a completed climb by noon. The primary reason: deadly lightning storms that are known to whip up quite suddenly from midday on in the Colorado Mountains.

Up and back by noon generally required our staying overnight at base camp and getting an early start in the morning. My son, Scott, and I had been climbing together for several years. Our goal was to climb each of the fifty-plus fourteen-thousand-foot mountains in Colorado.

I don't recall which number this was for us, but we had plenty of experience to know better than to handle the morning the way we did. We stayed in a motel near the mountain, left late, and hung around the base of Yale just goofing off together until 10:30. That was mistake number one.

The southeast route was a three-hour climb to the top and back. So even the fastest route, perfect conditions, and a very efficient climb would put us at the summit around noon.

As it turned out, the conditions *were* perfect. It was a gorgeous day and the crisp mountain air encouraged our quick steps. Even so, the climb up took a little longer than we expected. At 12:20, under a thinly overcast sky and no apparent threat of bad weather, we were about a hundred yards from the summit—mission nearly accomplished.

Scott was carrying a video camera and his walking stick. He was ten feet to my right when I heard him yell.

"Dad, my walking stick is humming!"

I turned and saw the hair on his head was standing straight up.

"Dad, the video camera is humming!" He looked around. "The rocks are humming!"

Then I felt the humming. And with the words of alarm barely out of Scott's mouth, sixty-mile-an-hour winds and hail exploded on us—no warning but the humming.

"Dad, we gotta get outa here!"

I looked up at Yale's summit and yelled back, "I'm going to the top to sign the canister first!"

And with that, I threw down my backpack and ran toward the top of Mount Yale. That was mistake number two.

2:00 PM, DAY EIGHT, HEATHROW TO BELFAST, FLIGHT BD86

Looking out the window with just about an hour left in the flight to Belfast, I could see the scene of Scott and me on Mount Yale as if watching it on a screen in vivid color and hearing it in surround sound. It came to mind while appreciating mountainous cloud formations, which turned to recollection of a lifelong fascination with mountains and development of a love for mountain climbing.

After several days of enjoying family time, relaxing, and exploring London and the surrounding areas by foot, train, boat, and taxi, I was ready to get back to work. Belfast was one of the locations I had most looked forward to when planning the tour.

The center of one of the mountain-size clouds lit up with crisscrossing lightning bolts, like filaments inside a light bulb.

How tall is that thing? I wondered, as I had many times in the past, mostly when flying one of my own small aircraft.

A thousand feet at the very least was my guess, given the absence of anything relative on which to base a better one.

It lit up again. Perhaps if a monument, like the Gateway Arch back home in St. Louis, were next to it in actual size, I would think differently . . . two, three, or even five thousand feet.

Maybe this was where the mountain climbing started, I thought, *all those early years flying throughout the Midwestern United States with Roger, passing through hundreds of miles of cumulous formations like birds through a mountain range.*

Climbing in elevation up the side of one of those giant formations can be a real eye-opener. Mountains and clouds have a way of making a person less ego-conscious. They're as glorious as they are massive. And as much as I have always enjoyed them from the ground view, staring down upon them from an airplane is a far more consuming experience. Like when you're looking into an aquarium of fish, twenty minutes can disappear before you know it. In a plane, that's the better part of St. Louis to Kentucky Lake.

I recalled Dad loading the family car and taking Mom, Roger, Karen, and me out west to see the Grand Canyon, Yellowstone, and the Snake River in Idaho. That was the mid 1940s. Terrell had not yet joined the family.

Dad's brother, Pete, lived in Montana, so we would travel through the northern Rockies to go see him. All that sightseeing was my first exposure to mountains.

As with just about everything else in my life, reading also had a big influence. I read a book called *Colorado Mountains*. In it was a chapter on the "Fourteeners." There apparently is some disagreement as to how many fourteen-thousand-foot peaks there are in Colorado, whether fifty-two or fifty-four. But it didn't matter much to me. There were fifty of them for sure, and the thought of climbing them all inspired me to at least get started and climb. The book told of a canister at the top of each mountain that each summiting climber signs, adding their names to the list of those who conquered the peak.

Since I'm accomplishment-driven, that especially intrigued me.

Scott and I began knocking a couple of mountains off a year when he was fourteen. We climbed eighteen of them before he got married and his family and job took precedence and our quest fizzled. But before it did, we got a lot of good climbing in.

We worked out a certain approach to it together. We agreed to do no technical climbing—no ropes, crampons, ice boots, or anything like that. It would generally go like this: We'd plan together for months, travel to Colorado, go to the REI store to get topographical maps and supplies, drive to the end of the road leading to the mountain, hike to a camp site (lakeside preferably) and set up camp.

The hikes usually took two to three days. With backpacks weighing fifty to sixty pounds, we would hike the entire second day, crossing meadows, streams, and snow fields. That stage alone was worth the trip. The day of the climb to the summit we would try to be on the trail by daybreak and down by noon to avoid the storms. Uncompahgre Peak was our first Fourteener.

Half the fun of the experience was the planning. Where would we go? What did we need to know about that mountain and the various routes to take to the top? What equipment did we need? What was the budget? How long would the trip take? How much fuel? How much food?

We were father and son, but also climbing companions depending on each other for thorough preparation, sharing responsibilities, and creating *OIMF!* long before arriving at the site of a climb. We spent weeks together before each climb getting into shape. We were a team.

While we climbed, we talked about life, values, and just whatever came to mind. We saw stunning scenery together.

Discipline affects every aspect of a climb, as it does all of life. We learned a lot about that together. Of course, the summit was the "high point" of it all—being at the top, the highest place around, signing the canister, taking pictures (the trophy of a climb), and creating incredible memories.

The Mount Yale memory was particularly poignant as I looked out the window and watched the interior of a bulbous cloud light up with lightning just about every ten seconds or so.

12:26, MOUNT YALE

After signing the canister, I turned to head down the mountain.

A hellacious lightning strike hit the ground nearby. It was crazy close.

Booming thunder repeatedly shook the ground, and one lightning strike after another rattled me. We were quite a ways above the tree line at the top of a mountain in the middle of an actual lightning storm—Scott and I were the tallest points around. The lightning strikes were all around us.

There was too much lightning. Too many bolts and blasts too close for them to keep missing. I expected at any second to be struck—a charred corpse amid blackened rocks at the top of Yale. For the first time in my life I was pretty sure it was my time.

I clearly remember the moment I said aloud, "God, if it's my time, I'm ready."

Seconds later I heard Scott's voice. He was reciting Psalm 23, "The Lord is my shepherd . . ."

Immediately in the middle of that mayhem an indescribable peace filled me, and I knew we would make it. The goal was to get below the tree line—to where trees would be the lightning rods instead of us. We moved as fast as we could, and it was as if thunder charged down the mountain after us. We could actually hear it rolling down the mountain from points of explosive violence.

Hail was still pounding when we slipped between the first trees. That was the last time we ever took our plans lightly or set out on a climb late. I am glad to be here to report it was not our last climb.

The Lord is my shepherd,
I shall not want.
He makes me lie down in green pastures;
He leads me beside quiet waters.
He restores my soul;
He guides me in the paths of righteousness
For His name's sake.

Even though I walk through the valley
Of the shadow of death
I fear no evil, for You are with me;
Your rod and Your staff, they comfort me.
You prepare a table before me
In the presence of my enemies;
You have anointed my head with oil;
My cup overflows.
Surely goodness and lovingkindness
Will follow me all the days of my life,
And I will dwell in the house of the Lord
Forever.

—Psalm 23

CHAPTER 8

BELFAST

TWO LARGER-THAN-LIFE SEAFARING STORIES are closely associated with Belfast.

One, the story of the *Titanic*, we know to be true. The other is a legend more than a millennium old. It is that of the Red Hand of Ulster, a grotesque tale of victory won in a boat race to claim rule of Northern Ireland—victory secured by the man losing the race until he lopped off one of his hands and hurled it to shore using his other, thereby touching land ahead of his competitor.

"The *Titanic*" would be a rare answer to the question, "What comes to mind first when you hear the name 'Belfast'?" Yet, there it stands in history: the shipyard home and fateful maiden voyage launch site of the most famous of all ocean liners.

Still, for most, "Belfast" calls to mind bloody conflict and societal tensions more symbolically represented by the Red Hand of Ulster.

Belfast is a city pregnant with the intrigue of contradiction. Modernization, the ubiquitous mark of Ireland's nearly forgotten Celtic Tiger financial boom, and lingering dark memories of "the Troubles" between Protestants and Catholics serve as strange identity for residents treasuring ancient associations and a region deeply rooted in pre-Christian histories.

The sensational imprint of riots, bombs, and terrorism decades in the past still scare away tourists but not immigrants. This densely populated urban landscape boasts one of western Europe's lowest crime rates.

Tall barbed wire fences, concrete barriers and wooden walls (twenty feet high in places) dressed with artistic tributes to famously political tensions divide Irish neighbors who all share the same reputation for warmth, hospitality, and good humor. Opposing sectarian brooding hides behind raised pints and carefully chosen words in hundreds of musically charged pubs central to the cultural currency of *craic* (good times!).

Conflict is complicated. Usually, to understand it you must have an archaeological determination—a look way back and some unearthing. Otherwise it becomes impossible to make sense of current, ongoing hatred where present causes of worthy proportions are hard to find.

Easy labels, such as "religion," simply won't do. These labels are hollow where bloody red hands, opposing flags, and political slogans are more commonly flaunted than scripture references, crosses, and crucifixes; where political control meets determined independence; where freedom is somewhere in a fractured space between definitions and allegiances; when the titles "Protestants" and "Catholics" are interchangeable with "Loyalists" and "Unionists," or "Nationalists and Republicans," and further division has produced operating factions and political faces such as the Unionist's IRA, Real IRA and Sinn Fein, and the Loyalist's UDA, UDF, and UVF.

No, such long-lasting divisiveness comes from something much deeper than religious identities. Pains, harms, losses, humiliations, devastations, and brutal conquests have played out over the course of millennia. Evidence dominates a landscape recalling the need for castles with high walls of protection, which ultimately did not prevent their ruins. In Northern Ireland, historical chronology holds accounts of atrocities and horrors, offenses so great . . . offenses that are hard to let go of and move on from.

The question is not, "Why did religion cause people to behave so viciously?" but, "Why did the introduced religion not provide more than new titles under which territorial barbaric atrocities occurred?"

But that is a discussion for a bigger book than this one.

Even as memories of past difficulties linger, the people of Belfast fight a new battle; not a fight of "us" versus "them," but a fight for a new day, with peace and prosperity finding ways to thrive. Evidences of these are as plentiful as those of the past.

And *it is* Northern Ireland, after all. So, on any given afternoon peaceful scenic beauty is near. To the north, south, and west, relief from contradiction and conflict is emerald green, the constant of Northern Ireland hill country, and eastward deep blue, the North Channel of the Irish Sea.

This island just off of Europe's western shore is a gem of glorious beauty. Well, in the case of my visit, gray-green. It rained continuously.

7:00 PM, DAY EIGHT, LOUGH ERNE RESORT

Edmund Johnston picked me up at the Belfast airport and we drove to the site of the next presentation in a steady rain. I liked him immediately.

The chair of the Vistage group I would speak to the following day, he informed me something special was in store for the evening. The conference hall was located in the center of Lough Erne Resort just outside of Enniskillen in Fermanagh County, Ireland. Nick Faldo designed the course, and everything about the resort was equally world-class.

The dinner we enjoyed—all members of his group were present—was a memorable experience itself. But I sensed the "something special" was still to come.

No sooner were dishes removed from the tables than Edmund addressed the group I already felt part of. Each of the eighteen members had come prepared with an object that represented something very important to him or her. Edmund wanted everyone to leave this evening knowing something of every other person's heart. He felt this was an important preparation for my two presentation sessions the next day, which he hoped would significantly impact the entire group.

As each person stood and revealed his or her object, stories were told and explanations given. With over six hundred Vistage speaking engagements in my past, I had never had this experience. Vistage meetings are typically focused on business. My talk would be about life and personal priorities. The exercise would prove to be key to open the group for truly rich relational connections.

One man stood and held up a picture of his family, telling something about each person in the photo and giving background that left little doubt of his family's utmost importance to him. Another speaker held up a picture of his motorcycle. His tale of touring Europe on two wheels almost made me want to join him for an adventure. A fishing boat, a book, a journal of poems, and the Bible were among the inspiring artifacts presented that evening.

Thankfully, I had a special picture with me to proudly hold aloft when my turn came. Edmund had suggested in advance that I might come to dinner with an example of something precious to me. The assignment could not have been easier. It simply indulged a readiness for my favorite focus of bragging: Betty. After displaying the photograph of her, I was asked to share a story. Perhaps because of the influence of steady rain since my arrival, one in particular came to mind . . .

FRIDAY, 8:00 AM, MARCH 21, 1986

Rain was pouring when I opened the door of the small trailer, dressed in my professional best and ready to enter another day of cold-calling futility.

Or that's about where my head was. I was mostly discouraged, and though determined to make something of the day, had no indication in my favor that determination would produce any more action than all the blanks I had fired previously.

Rain had fallen all night—the world was soggy out there.

As I stepped onto the one stair between the trailer and the ground, my foot slipped and I was suddenly face down in the mud and leaves. Soaked from head to toe in the heavy rain, I lifted my muddy face and said out loud, "Dr. Hill, you have lost your mind!"

Other mutterings followed while I got to my feet. "You had a comfortable job you couldn't get fired from, a good salary with excellent benefits, professional respectability, and money in the bank. And you walked away from it all for what?"

I had announced my resignation at the University of Missouri in February 1986. After cashing out my retirement, selling all but a few personal items put in storage, and paying off all our debt, I met with family and a few close friends for breakfast at Country Kitchen in Columbia before heading out on the adventure the morning of March 9.

It was a tearful breakfast, to say the least. Betty stayed behind to oversee the sale of our house and get Scott through the final weeks of his junior year of high school. It was just me, a pickup, a camper, and the clothes on my back.

I arrived in Atlanta later that day and met with my new business partner, Howard, before parking the camper in a trailer park next to Fort Gordon. The next day Howard and I met in Augusta to spend the day cold-calling. I had received no training on selling franchises. It was Monday, March 10. To that point, one week of training as a franchisee at the RE/MAX international headquarters in Denver was the extent of my preparation.

Howard said, "Good luck!" and headed back to Atlanta.

I am not sure I could have started with a greater confidence level. Selling a terrific product, backed 100 percent by a wonderful wife, sporting a knock-'em-dead attitude, and having opportunity calling my name, it was a "can't miss" situation to my thinking. Betty and I were both fifty years old, but we felt and thought like twenty-year-olds.

RE/MAX had what they called the "100 percent concept." In traditional real estate offices the broker and the agent split sales 50/50. The broker paid for the office and advertising. With RE/MAX, the agents got 100 percent, paid for their own advertising, and paid the broker a fixed fee per month to work out of that office. Most agents wanted to be owners, so it was an attractive arrangement.

Competition is the name of the game in sales. Thus I had two types of prospects: independent brokers that wanted national brand recognition for competing against other national real estate agencies, and top producing agents who were tired of paying brokers 50 percent of their sales.

With the RE/MAX system, the first sale of the month covered expenses, and all others after it were gravy. On March 11, my official on-my-own start date, I was almost giddy with optimism.

It took just ten days to go from pumped to deflated. On March 21 I had yet to accomplish a single appointment with a prospective buyer. I was getting an education in excuses. A meeting scheduled turned out to be a meeting canceled or postponed for one reason or another every time.

The product I thought was so exciting turned out to be a repellant of interest. One agent sarcastically said, "Now tell me again . . . you're with Relax? You're a mattress company or what? What are you selling?"

Pulling my ego-damaged self up out of the mud that fine Friday morning, I was totally conflicted. My former prestigious doctoral position overseeing many professional subordinates was looking like the kind of success to which everyone aspired—one that only a crazy man would turn his back on.

Obviously education was my strong suit, *not* sales. With a wealth of credentials and experience, a teaching position somewhere was a viable and attractive option to me. Before I had resigned my position at MU I had agreed to teach a two-week course for Extension Services at Ohio State University in Columbus, Ohio. That date was coming quickly, and I was once again excited about teaching and being around people who were interested in what I had to say.

The hardest part was actually being away from Betty and the rest of my family and feeling totally alone in the adventure. Emotionally I was at the bottom. Even so, a full day remained ahead of me, so I cleaned up, got redressed, and headed to a scheduled meeting I hoped would be my first to actually *take place*. But it was not long before I realized I was lost.

Stopping in to a business near where I thought I was supposed to be, I met someone willing to help direct me to the location of the meeting. His name was Ken, and to my surprise, he was genuinely interested in the reason for my meeting.

I gave him my RE/MAX pitch, and he was impressed. It was a start. I didn't know that he would turn out to be one of my first franchisees.

The two-week teaching break could not have been more perfectly timed. Cold-calling "reality," rejection, and depression of a magnitude I had never encountered had been more than enough challenge for the time being. Columbus sounded like paradise. More importantly, it gave me the chance to step back and reevaluate things, knowing I could not afford to be double-minded about this. I was either going for it or not.

Rejuvenated at the end of the break, I no longer felt any wavering in my commitment. Before long Betty joined me in Georgia and my focus was laser sharp. The original vision—be successful enough at this to one day own the RE/MAX rights to an entire state—was again our focus. It ended up being important that I faced those first days alone. I fought my demons alone and won. But Betty, my inspiration, was back at my side, and I was more inspired than ever.

Sometimes the best way to communicate the importance of nearness and intimacy is through memories of when they are absent—tales of the desert.

It seemed so in the case of my mud puddle story. From that point on everyone in the group treated me as if they had not only met me but met Betty *and* me at the dinner party that night. One little photograph accompanied a five-minute story that Betty was mostly *not* in. And, of course, that was the point, which they really seemed to get. It always surprises me that such ordinary things can have so much power. But then, we live mostly in the ordinary, don't we? It turns out to be a rather easy place to meet each other.

It is like the high E in Beethoven's "Fur Elise." The lovely—almost universally recognizable—melody dominates, supported by the back and forth between A and E chords, then the C chord and on to a run up the keyboard like the rushing waters of a babbling brook until the E 7th and, as a single droplet leaping over the banks and out into some soulful place we all know of but cannot name, the high E splashes, bursting open and laughing with delight.

Completely absent from the famous melody, yet somehow implied like rumor all through it, when the note is touched it is never again forgotten. It becomes that anticipated treasure in the music, that magical moment (Beethoven's genius is time) for which the melody *exists*.

So often I am traveling, giving talks, and meeting with people in situations where the notoriety is mine for books, presentations, stories, principles, and success, while Betty is somewhere else impacting the world with her own busy and abundant life. But when she is introduced—if even by photograph and story—the name Tom Hill cannot be spoken or heard without her defining, unforgettable presence completing the thought.

Maybe it was the sharing of my mud puddle story and the picture of Betty. Maybe it was the accumulated impact of the many personal stories we shared that night. But when I headed back to my room after it was all over, I knew without a doubt that lifelong friendships had been born, and that I am one wealthy man!

If I set the sun beside the moon
And if I set the land beside the sea
And if I set the town beside the country
And if I set the man beside the woman
I suppose some fool
Would want to talk about
One being better.

—G. K. Chesterton

CHAPTER 9

SEEING

The rain had fallen all day, and by the looks of the dense, low gray canopy above, no letup was near. The morning session had proceeded smoothly. Breakfast and coffee were props supporting the general eagerness for more connection time.

After that, I devoted the first two hours to teaching the six life priorities, ended by Q and A that was more like a group discussion. Interest in the subject matter was lively.

With a ten-minute break to stretch our legs, we were back at it. The topic shifted to G-curves—background and fundamental aspects of practice. Before the lunch break I wanted to get in a word or two of clarification concerning reasons, motivation, and vision. Knowing my audience, I began with an example:

> Peter Drucker, in his book *Management Challenges for the 21st Century*, tells about the reformist John Calvin and Ignatius of Loyola, a leader in the Counter-Reformation movement and founder of the Jesuit Order. Completely independent of one another at about the same time in the sixteenth century, they both implemented goal-setting rules for every member of their religious communities. Drucker proposes this as the reason followers of these two leaders dominated Europe

within thirty years—Calvinism in the Protestant north and the Jesuit Order in the Catholic south.

Principles of goal setting are all about seeing. They are blind to allegiance and bias, serving no favorites in terms of efficacious privilege. But they are clear and far vision for those who employ them and apply them with unyielding commitment—for those who have no regard for how contrary the beliefs and intentions.

Written goals are exacting and have a natural basis of accountability. It is impossible for goals to exist without motivation. Think about it—if not the result of some desirable outcome, why would a goal be stated . . . to what would it be connected?

This is exciting! A goal is set as an initiative directly supporting something you want. Yet, for some reason, many people avoid goal setting, thinking of it as technical or cumbersome. Some people apparently think their needs should be automatically met and their wants will just automatically materialize. They rarely get what they want.

Goal setting is the best way to "ask" for what we want. It is forming the question well, with clarity about the subject and conviction concerning the object of our desires. Goals aligned with our passions and core values and written down provide clear vision for where we are going and when we intend to arrive at that destination.

So what is the enemy of goal setting? Easy, right? Negative attitude and unbelief. It is amazing how much of this we lug around, not recognizing the real influence sabotaging our *right* to be goal setters and difference makers taking charge of our lives and going where *we intend*.

That is why goals are so important: they root out negative attitudes and foundations of disbelief. You have to confront these and identify them just to come up with an effective goal. You have to resist contrariness. And goals are the words of the sentence saying, "This is how I will get this done."

It doesn't do any good, however, to trivialize the enemy. So let's take a minute and look honestly at some of the substance behind negative attitudes and disbelief. Then let's look at the counterparts—the attitudes that encourage people to set lofty goals. Two words will serve as categories for the opposing attitudes:

"Victim" and "Victor."

In terms of symbols, these are barely even different. If you weren't familiar with them, you could at a glance expect them to be similar in meaning. But what a difference endings can make! Just two letters and . . . wow, worlds apart!

You might want me to demonstrate the validity of the prefix Dr. in front of my name by getting into the etymology or definition complexities of these two words for the sake of really understanding how different they are. No need. A casual look at other words we would all associate with each indicates their profound polarization.

Victim: fear, anger, imprisoned, contempt, spite, blame-shifting, excuses, caution, inaction, hostage, poverty (in every form), desperation, self-focused, entitled, irresponsible, resentful, negative, unforgiving, etc. Victor: freedom, positive, responsible, selfless (others-focused), boldness, action, accountable, blessed, thankful, celebratory, prosperous, (the) present, love, generous, forgiving, etc.

That reminds me—while we are on this linguistic focus, we really must talk about one other word: "forgiveness." Is anything more important? Honestly, can you think of anything more important? Anything more essential to personal liberty? Anything more foundational to peace? Any single thing more connected to your physical, mental, emotional, and spiritual health? Anything more central to well-being, to wholeness?

Think of a difficult relational situation characterized by forgiveness and identify the emotions associated with it. Do the same with a situation characterized by unforgiveness. Now *there's* some homework that will motivate at least a few people to some life-changing action.

But here's the misunderstanding: most people think of forgiveness as applied per incident of offense. You know . . . forgive the "idiot" for that idiotic thing he or she did to me yesterday. But what about the next offense, and the next, and on and on?

What about forgiving the idiot for being an idiot? What if I have some selfish idiotic tendencies that don't go away after one forgive-and-forget interaction between us?

I walked toward a new friend of mine seated in the nearest chair.

"Can I tell you a secret? I do have some of those tendencies. Can you please forgive me for *that*?" He reached out and we shook hands.

OK, before we move on, let's discuss one more attitude comparison I think we will all find pertinent. This is more of a conceptual comparison between attitudes concerning the times we live in. Here is the first one:

"There is so much struggle and difficulty in the world today, so many ways to go wrong, so many temptations, so much corruption, immorality, meanness, rudeness, crudeness, disrespect. We're just constantly blindsided by new health threats . . . bombarded with trash of every kind—media, violence, wars, politics, addictions, you name it. I don't know how anyone raises a family nowadays. And God help the kids growing up in this mess! Can you imagine what it will be like a generation from now?"

I walked about ten feet, stood in the middle of the gathering, and slowly turned, perusing the faces in my audience before reading the next statement.

"I don't think there has ever been a better time for developing great . . . really deep character. There are new kinds of challenges every day to test a person, to define one's values, to force us to clarify our thinking, strengthen our beliefs. There are more environmental demands for heroes, more brokenness to inspire healers and solution makers, more downward force of gravity for building those resistance muscles than at any time I can remember.

"Just speaking from my own experience, opportunities to make a difference and stand out and impact the next generation are constantly coming at me from every direction. Honor and nobility and righteousness just seem to stand out more. I see some young people coming up behind me that are, frankly, much deeper and more exceptional than I was at their age. I can hardly wait to see the impact they will have on their generation and the next. I hope I live long enough to see much of the exceptional lives they will live."

Which disposition best represents yours?

I prefer seminars for one main reason: the opportunity to get to know people. I enjoy people. I also have an insatiable appetite for their stories. There is an especially personal enhancement to delivering information when a person is speaking to his or her friends, however recent your meeting. Time between sessions is time for listening—invaluable to effective teaching.

In real estate it's *location, location, location!* With coaching and public speaking it's *connection, connection, connection!*

In this case, the connection was so special I was beginning to wonder if perhaps there was a bit of Irish in my family genes I did not know about. Touched by the warmth and acceptance shown to me right within the camaraderie of the group, it would have been easy to extend the lunch break another hour or two. But we had work to do.

We were talking about goal setting, if you recall, and the fact that goals clarify and expand vision. We talked about G-curves (eighteen-month goals) and quantum leaps (major goals accomplished in short periods of time). Quantum leaps are the result of applied goal-setting skills, activation of the laws governing human behavior on your behalf. But it is helpful to identify stages to the G-curve.

The first stage is *seeing possibility*, which is kind of like the "honeymoon phase" where anticipation of success and ultimately making a significant change comes into focus. That is the first six months.

The six- to ten-month phase is what I call the *incubation* period. This is when progress seems to crawl. Even though activity occurs, nothing appears to be happening. Here is where the goals are so important. Like a pilot trusting the instruments and not what he perceives or feels, it takes some internal fortitude to stay committed to the goals during this phase.

Just before the goals come to maturity there is a real test: the *breakpoint*. The mud puddle story I told you last night was mine. The test will challenge everything you have in terms of staying power. Too many people give up at this bleak moment. If you stop here, you will be discouraged and may even decide goal setting does not work. But trust me—staying committed and seeing it through will be worth it.

Halfway through the afternoon I gave everyone a half-hour break. Usually, I keep breaks to ten or fifteen minutes because of the challenge of getting all the material covered. But something was on my mind and distracting me—something I needed to go process alone.

The rain continued. So did the golf. Standing in front of a wall of windows staring out at the golf course, I was amazed to see Irish golfers who were unfazed by rain. By all appearance, the course was having a booming business day and the golfers showed no signs of distraction or irritation.

A short distance from the clubhouse was a helipad. It looked like a good *pondering pad* to me. I figured, *If the golfers can golf in a steady rain, the watcher can watch in it too.*

So, out to the helipad I went.

Turning slowly, I perused the scenic surroundings. Golfers everywhere enjoyed their craft and one another.

Golf . . . what's the magic in it? Not being much of a golfer, the question genuinely puzzled me. It also helped me realize what had been bugging me. *It's not the golf. It's the people.* I glanced around again slowly. It seemed surreal that I was smack in the epicenter of a part of the world famous for hostility.

These people? How is it even possible? These are some of the warmest, humblest souls I have ever encountered. I could not think of a time I had felt more welcomed or observed people respond to each other with more delight.

It was as if I were looking beyond the intoxicating Irish landscape, beyond the beautiful people and hilly horizon, right across to other places in the world famously torn by conflict. Was it this way there also? If I made a visit, would I find a warm welcome, generous hospitality, effortless connection, and easily flowing laughter?

I could not keep the tears from falling. It was OK—I was standing in the rain.

Keep your thoughts positive because
your thoughts become your words.

Keep your words positive because
your words become your behaviors.

Keep your behaviors positive because
your behaviors become your habits.

Keep your habits positive because
your habits become your values.

Keep your values positive because
your values become your destiny.

—Mahatma Gandhi

CHAPTER 10

MAPPING AND TIME

2:40 PM, DAY TEN, SURREY COUNTY

Boarding the Virginia Water train was beginning to feel a comfortable part of my daily life. From Virginia Water I headed to Clapham Junction where a quick exchange had me on another train to Vauxhall. From there it was the Victoria Line—Underground—to Kings Cross.

From Kings Cross trains depart every thirty minutes for Leeds Central. Thirty minutes is not a lot of time when you are a foreigner figuring out the system and going through a line to get a ticket.

Of course, the other way of looking at it is: Had I missed the train it was only thirty minutes until the next one. That strikes me as inefficient, so missing the train was not in the schedule. Two and a half hours later I was taking a taxi from the train station to Wood Hall Hotel and Spa on Trip Lane, in Linton, on the west side of Wetherby, a town within the metropolitan borough of Leeds, in West Yorkshire County, northern England.

With a long private drive reminiscent of Gliffaes Country House in Wales, Wood Hall Hotel sits atop a tall hill overlooking rolling hills of lush green as far as the eye can see. The stately mansion is all stone dressed in English ivy.

We pulled up to the impressively welcoming entryway, round with tall stone pillars. The back courtyard looks upon English landscaping so beautiful it challenges the imagination. Inside is elegance and more elegance, everywhere statements of refinement, many of them in that fine art of understatement, allowing for *enough said*.

But the most remarkable and enjoyable aspect of Wood Hall, for a man of academia like myself, was the grand history of its buildings and grounds. The River Wharfe (most prominent feature of Wetherby) runs directly through the hotel property. When originally built (twelfth to thirteenth century) the mansion was a country home of the Malgar Le Vavasour family and was situated directly on the banks of the River Wharfe.

The Vavasours were prominent nobles—so prominent that their family history spills over into legends of the period. The true-life romance of Maud and Fulke Le Vavasour bears striking resemblance to that of Robin Hood and Maid Marion. Maud and Fulke Le Vavasour's relationship is the subject of a chapter in Maureen Keen's book *Outlaws of Medieval Legend*, followed by several chapters on Robin Hood.

Passed from generation to generation of Vavasours for several hundred years, the original estate was destroyed by Oliver Cromwell's troops during the civil war of the mid 1600s, and much of the masonry was cast into the river. The mansion was rebuilt in the 1750s in its current location on the one-hundred-plus-acre grounds, much of the stonework rescued from the watery grave.

Proudly displayed in the front hall of the hotel is the York coat of arms. Since its reconstruction, the mansion has been the Scott family estate (for one hundred fifty years), a prep school for boys, the first pastoral and ecumenical center in Britain (owned by the diocese of Leeds, Mother Teresa of Calcutta among the first visitors), host to Vietnamese boat people arriving after the Vietnam War, and a hotel since 1988.

Like a stone patchwork quilt, the complex includes outhouse facilities from the Vavasour era (the dining room), cottages built in the 1600s during the reign of James I, an array of stables and outbuildings, and recent additions for spa accommodations. As if signature to the peaceful, contemplative environment, in the realm of the hotel a Carmelite monastery (home to a silent order of nuns) is a place of worship for anyone who chooses. With more history and personality than any building I can recall visiting, every corner of the place was a wealth of fascination and fodder for conversation.

Day 11, Bowcliffe Hall, Wetherby, Leeds

This was the city-to-city, day-to-day, busy section of the tour. Everything was running like a Rolls-Royce—smoothly. I had surprisingly few kinks to work out in the early presentations—mostly just getting used to different audience types and figuring out how to read them and make adjustments for optimal communication and impact.

It is amazing how much difference a body of water or a few miles can make in the way people relate to one another. Surrey, Powys, Belfast, Wetherby . . . every Vistage group is as unique as the region in which it meets. Like the marathon I had run in Greece before the Olympics a few years earlier, strong preparation and execution simplified focus to fluid stride and enjoyment of the experience.

Bowcliffe Hall was a twenty-minute taxi ride from Wood Hall Hotel. The Wetherby group was fifteen in number and each person the value of ten in energy. There was a feeling of fun in the atmosphere, making it easy to plunge in and move through the presentation. Before I knew it, time was nearly expired. And *Time* was also the point we were at in the Exceptional Life map.

> Goal planning is about mapping, and central to mapping our goals is time. Yes, goal planning is focused on execution of tasks, development of new skills, building important relationships, overcoming obstacles, accomplishing missions, taking steps, following up, and so on. But every one of those takes time. Remember, we are not just talking about accomplishments; we are talking about the Exceptional Life. The overarching design of a goal map aligned to core beliefs is organization insuring all six of our life priorities are built

into planning. They can be measured—must be measured—and controlled in terms of time. That is why our lists are so essential: lists maximize efficiency and *create* time. The statement, "I don't have time to make a list," is a stranger to the reality of a list's primary value.

Think of it in terms of music. Absolutely every mark on a sheet of music conveys something about time—every mark! Imagine the music was not written down, not organized on treble and bass clefs, not communicated on a page at which we could look. The musicians all come together to work on a piece of music, and everything has to be discussed, explained in order for each instrument to be coordinated with the next—in time.

Time is a reality being handled, just extremely inefficiently. What could be accomplished in an hour if the music were written, instead takes days, maybe longer. It is the same with goal mapping.

Time is a strange animal. We all have the same sixty seconds in a minute and sixty minutes in an hour, twenty-four hours in a day, seven days a week, and three hundred and sixty-five days a year. Why do some people get so much more out of them? How is it we talk about *making* time and *building* time? Why do people who *spend* time setting goals and *take* time writing them down wind up with more of it? Why are *they* the ones, for example, taking the best vacations? They *plan to*. They write out the plan in measures of time, and make it work. It is that simple.

When they need to delegate responsibility or schedule solitude for spiritual and emotional well-being, they recognize it because it is on the map, rather than doing it as a reaction to crisis. When they need to clone themselves to be in multiple places at once, to learn about technologies and resources and develop new skills to help do that, they know because the plan requires it. They manage these in measured time that reasonably fits into daily, weekly, and monthly lists.

We want to think differently about time, to think of ourselves as time professionals and of time in terms of resource, stewardship, expertise, craft, and product.

Time is the most valuable thing we have. From Aristotle to Einstein to Hawking, time is at the center of every discussion of the nature of our universe. How can we evaluate it accurately, multiply it, cultivate it, make the most of it? Goal mapping, plans, lists . . . these are steps of responsible ownership of time management.

I'll give you a little exercise to help you appreciate just how much time is wired into the nature of who we are as humans. This is for your alone time, for some intentional time of solitude, something just to bless you.

Spend some time listening to baroque music at largo tempo. It is recorded at eight to twelve cycles per second, the same as alpha waves in the corpus callosum, which processes electrical and chemical messages passing between the right and left hemispheres of the brain.

The left side functions at twelve-plus cycles per second, called beta waves, and the right at four to eight cycles per second, called theta waves. The left side is the logical, conscious side of the brain, and the right is the subconscious, creative and intuitive side.

The alpha waves in the corpus callosum are harmonizers in the processing between the two. Listening to baroque music at largo tempo—recorded at the same eight to twelve cycles per second as the alpha waves—encourages harmonious connection and enhances the creative process. Try it. I can't prove it or explain it any more deeply or scientifically than that, but I know it works.

The point is: whether at the level of alpha, beta, and theta waves and cycles per second, or one day, a ninety-day plan, six-month plan, eighteen-month plan, thirty-six-month plan, or six-year plan, *time matters* and we can influence it in our favor and for our best interest and that of others around us. If there is a key to Designing Your Exceptional Life, it is managing time.

As time does when things are at their best and flowing smoothly, it flew by and was at an end. Thinking we could sneak in a few quick questions, I made the invitation. But the first question was actually a reminder—that I had left them hanging just past the mud puddle phase of my RE/MAX journey. I looked at my watch, remembering I had a plane to catch.

"OK, I'll do my best," I said. "But this will take more than a couple of minutes and for sure the rest of our time together."

After a moment of thought, I remembered just where to start . . .

Time is a created thing.
To say "I don't have time,"
is like saying, "I don't want to."

—Lao Tzu

Time is an illusion.

—Albert Einstein

Yesterday is gone,
Tomorrow has not yet come.
We have only today.
Let us begin.

—Mother Teresa

CHAPTER 11

MOMENTUM

MAY 6, 1986, SOUTH GEORGIA

Shortly after my moment of truth mud puddle experience came the two-week interruption for teaching at OSU in Columbus, Ohio—both of which were perfectly timed in the overall orchestration of things, as was the struggle of getting started alone.

While I was in Columbus, my team had arrived. Brett Blair, an engineer, and Vicky Miserez, a former 4-H associate at the University of Missouri, had decided to be a part of the journey as prospectors and were finally able to join me in Georgia. While I was in Ohio they had begun their work snooping around for solid prospects, and I was receiving encouraging reports.

In early May I sold my first franchise. It was to a couple of guys who already owned one RE/MAX franchise and, discovering we were in the area selling them, decided they did not want any competition. So they bought a second one to protect their locale.

I did not care what the reason was. It was a start. And that start added *hunger for more* to already growing tensions in my mind. The $36,000 retirement cash-out would not support us for much longer. A month and a half in and *one sale* . . . the situation was still feeling a bit sketchy.

Then came what I regarded as disastrous news. Sears had purchased Coldwell Banker and was installing offices in all stores nationwide. Knowing little about business, I could not have had more of a rookie reaction. As if standing engulfed in shadow at the base of the Sears

Tower in Chicago, my thoughts were bug-size: *I risked everything on an upstart brand nobody knows about and now a big national company like Coldwell Banker teams up with Sears? We're toast!* I thought.

Truly scared, I went to see a veteran real estate agent to see what chances he thought anyone else in the industry had of survival.

"Tom, I think we will be OK," he said.

"Really . . . why?"

I will never forget his answer.

"Well, Tom, I went to Sears to see what was what with CB in their store. When I got there, I needed to ask where it was. A lady pointed and said, "See the pantyhose down at the end of that aisle? Turn left there, proceed to the bras, and you will see it off to your right.""

Before leaving his office, I thanked him for the new perspective. Sure enough, the experiment did not last long and Sears sold Coldwell Banker.

After selling the camper trailer, Betty, Scott, and I moved into a tiny condo on an island near Savannah. My weekly sales approach was very methodical: every Monday morning I picked out a small town in southern Georgia and headed there in my Ford Ranger pickup to try and sell a franchise. Arriving at the town, I selected a motel for a base of operations and a bed for the week.

Driving across South Georgia on May 6, a nice sunny day, I felt a lot of pressure to generate sales. Something in the sky caught my attention, and I looked up to see what appeared to be reflection from an airplane.

I looked at it, wondering what kind of plane it was. Then I realized there was no plane. It was just a bright light.

A peace came over me as if I were being baptized in the light. It was deeply calming. Though not in an audible voice, a message came to me: "Relax, I've got you."

I knew it was going to be OK.

July 1986, Savannah, Georgia

The average person selling RE/MAX franchises nationwide was selling one a quarter. By July my team had sold eight—eight in two quarters, and we had not gotten going until the second quarter! I was the number 1 RE/MAX salesperson in the country!

That was the good news. Not so good was the fact that we had exhausted our opportunities in outstate Georgia. A full franchise in a heavily populated area sold for $15,000. A franchise in a smaller town was as low as $2,500. I was supporting a team, not just myself, so the motivation to pour it on was high.

I called Howard to see what I could do next. Atlanta was not an option—it was his, and he was not offering to share. He called Dave Liniger, the owner of RE/MAX, to see if he would sell us the rights to a state. The answer was "No."

We were meeting an obstacle none of us had foreseen, especially so soon into the journey.

In August we decided it was best to move to Atlanta to be closer to Howard and strategize. We got an apartment and were there two weeks when Dave Liniger called and said Kentucky and Tennessee had come up for sale.

I will never forget Howard's words: "They're going to let us buy them!"

We all broke into a celebration of hugs and kisses. That was our dream! From the very beginning, the whole reason Betty and I had taken Howard's challenge to come on board with RE/MAX was for the chance to own the rights to an entire state. That was our goal, and we had already gotten there.

By mid-August, the paperwork was done, and we were the proud RE/MAX owners of not one but *two* states. So we loaded up the truck and moved to Tennessee. . . . Yes, it did seem a little Beverly Hillbillies-ish.

My daughter, Terri, had joined us by then, So Betty and I, with Terri and Scott, moved into an apartment in Nashville over Labor Day weekend 1986. Between March 10 and September 5 we had lived in a camper trailer, a condo on an island near Savannah, an apartment in Atlanta, and an apartment in Nashville. What an adventure!

The journey to that point had cost us everything we had made. So with no money, we were starting from scratch once again. Howard worked some numbers and told me I needed to sell ten franchises by Christmas in order to make it. Because we could not afford an office, our two-bedroom apartment (complete with temporary furniture—we slept on futons) would have to serve as living and work space.

Every night I would do calisthenics beside my bed, to which I would repeat over and over in rhythm, "I'm gonna sell ten franchises."

Every morning it was the same, waking up in the dark, doing calisthenics, and reciting, "I'm gonna sell ten franchises," just pushing that down into my subconscious.

After the exercises it was time to get out the white pages. I would set them on the table and say to myself, "Tom, there are a million people here in the Nashville area. I will meet every one of them if I have to."

As for the rest of the team: Vicky Miserez moved to Nashville with us, while Brett Blair moved to Louisville and worked for me from there until taking a job with Alcoa, which eventually brought him to Nashville as well.

After working in the tight confines of southern Georgia, the entire states of Kentucky and Tennessee seemed pretty wide open. We had also become confident in our methods as a team. By December 3 I had sold nine franchises and needed just one more to make my goal. But I did not have a single prospect.

On December 4 I received a call from Kingsport, Tennessee—from out of the blue, as they say. It was a lady who owned a small real estate company.

"You don't know me, but I've done my due diligence, and I have a check waiting here for you," she said.

By Christmas the goal Howard had challenged me with was met; I sold exactly ten franchises.

In February 1987 Howard called.

"Tom, Southwest Ohio is for sale—Cincinnati, Dayton . . . Do you want to buy it?"

The price was $150,000. I told him I didn't have any money.

"If I buy it and give you 49 percent of it, will you run it for me?" he asked.

One state was the dream. We had already exceeded the dream by one.

There was no need to think about an answer. I said, "Where do I sign?" Betty and I were the owners of two and a half states.

Shortly afterward, I met an attorney. He said, "Kentucky, Tennessee, and Southwest Ohio are yours. Do you know if there are any other states for sale?"

The Dixie region—Alabama, Louisiana, and Mississippi—was for sale.

"Are you going to buy it?" he asked.

"No, we're all out of money," I answered.

He immediately asked, "How much?"

After looking into it I told him, "$150,000 cash."

He got back to me a short time later: "If I put up the $150,000 cash, will you give me 20 percent ownership?"

We were soon to be partners and owners of five and a half states. It is amazing the doors that open when people know you are a hard worker and one who sets and accomplishes goals.

That year I put sixty-six thousand miles on my car managing our five and a half states. One day I received a call from Vicky Miserez. She said, "I have a great prospect for you in Knoxville."

The man's name was Rich Levenson. I went to his office, cold call. It turned out he managed a traditional eighty-agent office and worked seventy to eighty hours a week for the owner.

We agreed to meet for coffee the next day. I did not know that the previous day he had asked that owner for the use of a Blue Book kept in his desk. Rich was trying to help his mother-in-law figure out the value of a car she was trying to sell.

The man had pulled the book out of the desk and thrown it at him saying, "Get your mind on your work!"

It was gnawing at him that he worked seventy to eighty hours a week for this man and was being treated that way.

When we met for breakfast at Shoney's restaurant, the timing could not have been better. I discovered the new acquaintance was one of the most interesting people to ever cross my path. Rich was a good storyteller, and I enjoyed hearing about his football exploits at the University of Miami, from which he transferred to play for the Tennessee Volunteers.

Just making a Division One college football team was exploit enough to my thinking. I knew this was a man of mettle. I told him about Betty and our family and a little of our story. He told me about his wife and how he had come to marry her. He was Jewish and she was a Baptist girl who had been engaged to another man. Rich had sold jewelry at the time and had a motor home for business travel. He was so in love with her that to prevent the marriage he invited her to talk in his motor home. Once she was inside, he closed the door, drove away, and did not stop until they reached the Dakotas.

"I kidnapped her," he said plainly. They married, had one son, and were nearing their thirtieth anniversary.

"Rich," I asked, "if you had a magic wand, what would happen?"

He pulled out his pen and, using it like a wand, struck his coffee cup, speaking to it as if it were his boss: "Conrad, you are a pile of crap!"

My calling on him turned out to be Rich's tipping point. In turn, his tipping point became mine. He quit his job, bought three franchises, became my best franchisee ever, and made me a ton of money.

No longer focused on survival or just managing five and a half states, the pilot in me took over and I was focused on soaring!

MAY 11, 1990, LOUISVILLE, KENTUCKY

For someone originally dreaming of owning rights to one state, owning five and a half was heady. But the constant travel was becoming more of a challenge. In the early going I didn't have a problem with driving at night, probably because of the excitement of getting started and tension of survival. That was becoming less the case, and fairly regularly I was finding it unavoidable.

Once, in late summer of 1989, on the interstate north of Birmingham late at night, I woke from a dead sleep, my hands resting on my lap, and the car traveling near 70 mph on the right shoulder of the highway.

For whatever reason, the steering wheel in that instant had moved back left, causing my vehicle to veer back toward my open lane, enough to barely miss a patrol car that had pulled someone over.

Plenty of times in my life I have needed a wakeup call. But I cannot recall a time when it was necessary to receive two.

In the fall of 1989 Betty and I decided it was time to try and sell Ohio and the Dixie region. Our thought was to buy Howard out of Tennessee and Kentucky, because we loved Nashville and wanted to stay there.

We approached him and he was adamantly against it. In May 1990 we were traveling to Bloomington, Indiana, to see our son-in-law, Eric Zinn, receive his MBA from the University of Indiana. We stopped in Louisville for the night and checked into a Hampton Inn.

At 2:00 in the morning on May 11, I woke with a vision—I say a vision because it was nothing like any dream I had ever had. It was in vivid color, sequential . . . like a documentary: (1) We sold our part of

Kentucky, Tennessee, and Ohio to Howard. (2) We bought Howard out of the Dixie states. (3) We moved to Jackson, Mississippi. (4) We let go of our team to make it work—fired them!—the team that had become two daughters and a son-in-law, replacements of Brett Blair (who got married and moved on) and Vicky Miserez (who had moved back to Columbia, Missouri).

I woke up feeling euphoric. It was so real, so clear. I knew it was the right thing to do. Well, the right side of my brain *knew*. The left side was not so sure. I lie there in bed analyzing the whole thing from a logical perspective. (1) No way on this green earth was Betty going to let me fire, lay off, or in any other form dismiss our three kids. (2) This was not anything Betty and I had ever talked about. We loved Nashville. We had bought some land—it was our home. *She* loved Nashville and was not about to leave for Jackson, Mississippi. (3) Howard was not going to go for this. He already owned majority interest, and I was doing all the work. Why, in his right mind, would he go for this? It was crazy! (4) We had just begun generating returns. There was no way the investor who put up the $150,000 to buy the Dixie region would go for this—if he did, he would want an outrageous amount of money!

The left side won.

"Get real, Tom!" was the verdict at that early hour of the morning.

Wide awake, I waited as long as I could before waking Betty to tell her about it: 5:00 AM. For two hours we talked about the points of the revelation. To my amazement, Betty said, "Let's go for it."

One obstacle, possibly the largest, was out of the way. At 7:00 I called Howard.

"Yeah, I'll be really interested in making that happen," was his response.

I was floored! We agreed that the biggest remaining issue was our investor friend, and Howard should be the one to call him. When he did, the man said, "You don't know how badly I need $150,000 right now. I'll sell it back to you for just what I invested."

Within two weeks of the 2:00 AM revelation, it was all completed. Within six weeks we were living in Brandon, Mississippi, an East Jackson suburb.

The years of sole ownership of the Dixie region were exceptional. Our son Scott was our company pilot, we enjoyed the south, and we came to love Brandon, just as we had Nashville. Yet, in 1993 we sensed it was time to move in a new direction. My mother was in her eighties and our kids were all starting families of their own. If we wanted to see them regularly, it was time to start thinking about selling the Dixie states.

In July we sold 25 percent to a RE/MAX owner named Dennis Curtin. Dennis had been the first RE/MAX franchisee outside of Colorado. He owned RE/MAX Arkansas, Oklahoma, Kansas, and Western Missouri. The agreement was that I would stay on as CEO for five years, at which time he would buy us out of the other 75 percent.

In January 1994 Dennis and I agreed it was best for him to run the Dixie region and I would simply retain 75 percent ownership until the five years was complete. My work with RE/MAX was over, and Betty and I moved back to Missouri where it had all begun.

It was all launched by decisions most thought I should reverse. Turning my back on status, stability and security, on many occasions the man in the mirror was the most critical, the biggest bully trying to get me to back down. Yet, the challenges along the way led to resolve and discovery of the authentic man inside.

What a journey!

One by one and two by two
lies are always biggest
but only one thing is true:
no matter how big you get
there's someone bigger than you.
So be your own man.

Golden sun and silver moon,
I don't need no silver spoon.
With my hands I'll tend my garden
and with them I'll eat my food.
I'll be my own man.

We walk through fire and we get burned,
life is hard and that's how we learn.
Before you spend a dollar
make sure another one is earned.
And be your own man.

—Matt Epp and Alex Sannie
My Own Man

CHAPTER 12

DREAMS AND DECISIONS

The entire history of the United States of America, even generously inclusive of the Colonial period, is held within a time frame from the beginning of the seventeenth century to the present—just over four hundred years.

In this history immigrants were overwhelmingly prominent. Wherever they set foot and sunk plow into earth, the English, French, Spanish, German, Dutch, Scandinavian, African, East European, and Asian people, among others, all built buildings and established societies contributing to the landscape.

Yet structural evidences of the first two hundred and fifty years are few and (literally) far between. Just a handful of churches, homes, and public buildings remain in visitor-worthy condition (mostly as museums and national monuments). Those remaining active in their original use—such as the White Horse Tavern in Newport, Rhode Island (1652), and Mission San Jose church in San Antonio (1720)—are of even greater rarity.

So appreciation of a massive building that has dominated a county landscape of northeastern England and remained in continuous use since its creation in the fourteenth century requires some mind stretching.

After setting a modest representation of belongings on the bed in my room at Lumley Castle Hotel, I sat for a moment and attempted to do just that—stretch my mind for an appreciation of six-hundred-plus years. Stumped, mainly due to distracted thoughts of Betty's well-being back in Virginia Water, I decided to go out and take in the view, one overlooking surrounding parklands, the River Wear, and the world-famous Durham County Cricket Grounds.

Sparkling in the progressing dusk, the lights of the town thinned to a star-like sprinkling in the sparse residential regions out toward the horizon. A sight to behold, but not one I was able to fully enjoy. I silently said another prayer.

The day began with the news that Betty had fallen back at the Zinns' home. She and Nina were preparing to go shopping in Richmond when she lost her balance coming down the stairs, fell, and badly hurt her tailbone.

Nina helped her to a sofa, where she remained in recuperation. I offered to cancel my Durham presentation and return immediately to the house, but Betty assured me she was doing fine in Nina's good care and insisted I not allow the mishap to mess up my plans as well as hers. Had I known the injury would keep her on the sofa for the rest of the trip and require a later trip to the A and E (emergency room) I would have been on the next train back to Virginia Water.

1:00 PM, DAY 13, HIGH GOSFORTH PARK, NEWCASTLE UPON TYNE

My morning run began as I descended from the castle, and it ended with a challenging but invigorating ascent of the hill on which the castle stands.

David D'Arcy, the Durham Vistage chair, "collected" me from the castle at 7:00 sharp and we proceeded to Marriott Gosforth Park where breakfast awaited and my talk followed.

After breakfast I called Betty, who assured me that she was about the same as the day before: sore but "OK," in good hands and confined to the sofa.

After spending the night in a six-hundred-year-old castle, a person's thoughts tend to move toward grand and lofty things. The experience influenced my presentation. The subject of dreams and dreaming unintentionally became an overarching theme in every phase of the talk—not involuntary dreams in one's sleep, but the *ability* to dream and dream big.

As I talked about the six life priorities, the dream topic emerged from each, and then from the values synergy of them all naturally came out as the *what* enabling a person to endure any *how*. When we got to the subject of goals and mapping, *the quality* of a dream just seemed to glow as motivation behind all the effort and bother. Finally dreaming forced its way front-and-center as the summation of the session, so I just went with it. The way it began might appear counterintuitive:

> Failure is critical. You have a famous cricket field down the road here and equally famous football, polo, tennis, and other sports venues all over your country. Some are brand new and here just because of the London Olympics. Anyone who ever set sights upon starring on one of those grand stages and *made it* failed regularly on the way there.
>
> In the US, baseball, football (North American style), and basketball are the big three. Babe Ruth is the greatest among the big names in the history of Major League Baseball—all-time home run king for most of a century. He also struck out more than anyone to ever play the game.
>
> Michael Jordan is the international giant of the game of basketball and also holds the dubious distinction of *missing over nine thousand* shots in his illustrious career.
>
> Brett Favre holds just about every meaningful record for touchdown passes in the history of the National Football League. As the all-time interception leader, with three

hundred and ten, he also outdistanced second place by thirty-three of those gifts to the opposition.

If we are not failing, we are not dreaming big enough to risk anything. If we are not losing ground here and there, it's because our dream is safe enough to ensure against setbacks.

If our hearts are never in danger, it is not because of perfection—it is because we did not bother to *care enough* to really *go for it!* With that kind of dreaming, sayings such as "Leave it on the field" would be irrelevant.

I am absolutely convinced that we cannot dream big enough dreams. I know some pretty good dreamers. I know some people who have made amazing dreams come true. But I don't know one person who is in danger of erring on the side of dreaming too big. We simply have way more capacity than we are prepared to exhaust.

Henry David Thoreau once said, "Most people live lives of quiet desperation."

Let me suggest three questions anyone can use to test the quality of a dream. One: What things in your life truly make you happy? Two: What are you committed to? And Three: What are you doing right now to use your full potential?

How you answer those will educate you about your heart and its investment.

Unfortunately, for most people the answers to these reveal no active dream and none even in development. For some this exposes dream avoidance. Yet, there is hope even in those revelations. What a helpful heads-up! Time to get on it, right?

For others there is a realization of the necessity to increase the grade of their dream. After all, the bigger question is: What is your future worth?

Another thing that can tell us volumes about what kind of dreamers we are and what kind of dreams we should be dreaming is taking a close look at our heroes.

I think I will just throw that out there as an assignment. Write your list of heroes, leaving room between for information about each.

A genuine hero is someone you admire enough to emulate. Be sure your list is made of genuine heroes, not people who merely impress you. Write down your heroes' values, as you perceive them. Write down actions and risks each has taken that demonstrate those values.

Remembering that these are *your* heroes, study that information and write down some things it says about you. Finally, go back to your dream and evaluate it on that basis. Does is represent who you are?

You see, dreams are made of heart and courage and reached by decisions. One of my favorite dream quotes is that of Johann Wolfgang Von Goethe. He said, "Whatever you can do, or dream you can, begin it. Boldness has genius, power, and magic in it."

I'll tell you two of my heroes.

They are from right here in your country: Winston Churchill and Margaret Thatcher. As leaders, they both valued education—they knew the importance of being well informed. They both cared about their generation enough to fight for it. Both faced perilous days and great opposition but believed they were the ones to get the jobs done. They believed they could inspire others and that others were worth inspiring.

Churchill once wrote to his mother: "I have faith in my star—that I am intended to do something in this world."

They both believed in the power of prayer and were not shy about calling on others to join them in it. That's because they both had big enough dreams to include the well-being of others ... dreams too big, in fact, to be accomplished solely on their own merits or by their own power. That's some quality dreaming.

Heroes like these teach me that every day we have a chance to show up and dream a big dream for someone and do whatever small or big thing it takes to make that happen.

There is nothing
With which every man
Is so afraid
As getting to know
How enormously much
He is capable of doing
And becoming.

—Søren Kierkegaard

I have missed more than
9,000 shots in my career.

I have lost almost 300 games.

On 26 occasions I have been
entrusted to take the
game winning shot . . . and missed.

I have failed over and over and over
again in my life.

And that's precisely why I succeed.

—Michael Jordan

CHAPTER 13

IN THE BLINK
OF AN EYE

Day 15, Virginia Water

It was good to be back at the Zinn home with Betty and the family and to be assured more directly that she was indeed "OK," even if not comfortable. She still had an inseparable relationship with the sofa Nina had delivered her to immediately after the fall.

Someone else might enjoy being waited on day and night. Not Betty. The greater pain for her was not being able to get up, not being able to accompany Nina on all those plans she had for showing her mom around the new environs. We were in England, and as much as she loved the Zinns' house, Betty was disappointed to see the same interior residential confines of the Royal land day after day.

The increasingly familiar and new favorite morning jog had again been my treat for two mornings. I was a little self-conscious about spending time out and about, in spite of Betty's encouragements to go make the most of the day and a half off from speaking, and the opportunity to be in the land of my ancestors. I did not like making the most of what Betty could make nothing.

My birthday happened to fall on the first of the days off. I spent it at Windsor Castle. Someone must have informed them of the big day, because upon arrival a grand parade was headed straight for me!

Splendid as advertised, the changing of the guard was precision at its best, a stark contrast to the remainder of the day, which was spent in aimless wandering at a very relaxed pace. I was able to see more of Virginia Water and Surrey County, a truly magnificent area—and more beautiful the more I saw of it.

Something about the transportation system (especially the trains) in England seemed to favor me. Perhaps it was designed for a left-brain-dominant fellow like myself—not too creative or complex, just straightforward and practical. I got around efficiently enough that I did not feel much like a visitor anymore.

On the itinerary for Day 15 was an afternoon flight to Edinburgh, sight of the next presentation. So I decided to get a haircut that morning and spend a few hours at the house with Betty before heading to the airport.

During the first week I was in Virginia Water, I had walked into a barbershop without bothering to ask about price. It's a haircut—all white hair, already short, nothing fancy—what could it cost?

Well, $60 was the shocking answer. I later discovered a trim at McBarber's in Egham, a town bordering Virginia Water, was $15. I headed over there.

A short time later, with a brief detour to swing by and see Hampton Court Palace, Henry VIII's little place, I returned to Lanscomb House on Nun's Walk, with Betty's coffee and some other goodies in hand.

I have learned over the years that Betty's smile is a study in understatement. Reading it is like pleasure in familiarity with Wordsworth, Napoleon Hill, or the Psalms. It has come to be one of the great delights of my life journey, though it has changed. And only I know the depths of those changes. There is courage in her smile. Not given to complaint, a person has to know the nuances of her smile to appreciate what she is thinking about the current moment in her own story.

12:15 PM, MARCH 1, 2011, LAKE ST. LOUIS, MISSOURI

Betty was with her friend Michelle Rowe at Max and Erma's. I was five minutes away at home. They had just sat down. The waiter walked up to the table to take their drink orders. When Betty tried to give hers, words would not come out. A few seconds later she fell over against the wall of the booth.

"You OK?" Michelle asked.

Betty could not answer.

A woman from the booth behind them immediately got into the booth with Betty, held her, and started asking questions: "Ma'am, what is your name? Ma'am, what day is it? Ma'am, what time is it? Where are you?"

She told her husband, "Call 911, she's having a stroke."

The lady was a nurse who had been going through stroke training. She was scheduled to be in class that morning, but the class was canceled so she and her husband decided to go out and have lunch together. She knew exactly what was happening and what to do.

Michelle called me, and I arrived as EMTs were putting Betty in the ambulance. She did not know who I was. Inside, an attendant asked, "Ma'am, what is your social security number?" Betty rattled it off perfectly. She did not recognize me but knew her social security number. *Hmm.*

When we got to the hospital they removed a blood clot. The doctor came out to speak with me and said Betty had suffered a severe stroke. She remained in the hospital for two weeks of rehab.

We had no warning, absolutely no indication that Betty was a stroke candidate ... just *boom!* ... there it was. We learned how precious good health is and how easy it is to take it for granted.

We learned once again that depending on others is part of the blessing of this life. We did not go through stroke training in some attempt to cover all the bases. But someone else had and she was right there when we needed her.

We have learned that life is not about ideal circumstances but how we react to the circumstances we face.

Some adjustments have been necessary for Betty and me. We enjoyed traveling quite a bit together; that has been cut back some. Our pace is a step slower day to day and our schedule lighter. Yet, progress has been steady and recovery remarkable.

Most importantly, Betty's joy and optimism are as high as ever, and my delight in her continues to increase. I don't know that God ever made a more positive thinker than the woman I married.

9:00 AM, Day 16, Edinburgh

I wish I could say it felt like Scotland. But it pains me to say that except for an abundant supply of the brogue I have always enjoyed, nearly everything in Scotland was rather *normal*.

Scotland is marked by glowing yellow highlighter (at least in the mind) on any itinerary, such as that of my speaking tour. I truly looked forward to this destination. Yet, such expectations forget the reality of brevity—I was there for less than twenty-four hours.

Edinburgh airport was, well, an airport. And travel from there to my hotel was in the dark, so the scenery looked like the interior of a taxi—just like one I'd ride in back home. I saw none of the country's magnificent landscape features. I would not have known it was seated on the coast of the North Sea if I hadn't seen that on a map.

My hotel, situated on the water and surrounded by statues, was exceptional, though I had little opportunity to explore it. Leaving at 7:00 AM, I saw its exterior by daylight only in the side mirror of a vehicle driving away from it as I was taken to the venue where my presentation would be. My conversation with my driver was so interesting I completely forgot to watch the scenery during that twenty-minute trip.

The Scots themselves saved my brief visit from that Hades of travel memory: "nondescript." I enjoyed dinner on the evening of my arrival with the Vistage chair of Scotland, Paul Pinson.

Paul was extremely interesting and intellectual. Admirably well read on a broad array of professional, technical, and cultural subjects, his knowledge was combined with evident genuine interest in others. A career in theater—a very big part of Edinburgh culture and its international fame—led to his founding an international theater company specializing in large outdoor productions.

But recently his career focus has shifted to more significant and demanding responsibilities with Vistage leadership, as well as mentoring as an executive coach through the Step Up program of the national cultural sector of Scotland.

The new career focus, he explained, is not so far from his previous work in theater. "Both share a concern for the human condition. In theater, all you have is story, and by it you explore human condition—who are we and where are we going? As an executive mentor coach, the invested concern is the same—not through fictional stories but through actual living persons. The subtext in theater is: what is the meaning behind the words? The subtext in coaching is: what is the meaning behind what we are accomplishing?"

How much each Vistage group reflects the chair always amazes me. In this case, Paul Pinson's leadership was evident not only in his rapport with the group members but also in the tight connection of the entire membership. The morning of the presentation began with each member saying a word or two about his or her career position and focus. Each was unique.

I am certain no other Vistage group to which I have spoken has been so generously endowed by youth. Numerous group members appeared to be in their thirties. And it was the only Vistage group in the world with a 50/50 gender split.

When you're addressing a gathering of highly successful professionals from Scotland's capital city, you think of the city's place in the world. As a major culture center of Europe and extremely significant during the Enlightenment, Edinburgh's intellectual influence helped earn it the nickname Athens of the North.

> I want to tell you about my brother. He had an odd symptom here and another there over a couple of weeks and decided to see a doctor. He did and some tests were taken. What the doctor said when he went in to discuss the results was a stunner. He had a rare disease called Creutzfeldt-Jakob disease, which is 100 percent fatal—not a single person has ever survived it. The doctor said its history suggests he had no more than three months to live.

> History was correct . . . almost to the day. What are the odds? A guy as healthy as could be going along minding his own business and *Hello!* Well, I can tell you the odds. The doctor told him that too: one in ten million.

> Those are not really the odds, though, are they? Those are just the numbers for how many in the overall population will get the disease. The odds for a given person being the one in the ten million to actually get it? Astronomical!

You might think a place known for its intellectual elite and close association with the Enlightenment would be a stop on the tour where one should tread lightly on the spiritual side of things. I did not have that sense at all. When presenting the six life priorities I stated forthrightly as always my conviction that our spirituality is the most important of all the priorities to have in order, supporting it with studies and statistics. They were as interested as the people are anywhere else I have visited, in part because of the universally pertinent question: What is the purpose of my life?

> The great contributors to spiritual thought from all over the world throughout history seem to hold one conviction unanimously: Life is about serving others.

I believe that to be true.

Creating is a big part of our spiritual nature. Where does abstract thought come from? What about the capacity to perceive, evaluate, discern a void of unique contribution and choose to fill it? Where does the belief that I *can* contribute creatively, or that my contribution matters come from?

If I were a gifted violinist, the son of a world-famous maestro, the question would be easily answered: *genetics.*

So how is the answer any different concerning our creating? Dad is *Creator*, after all.

From there, one life priority flowed right into another, and if no one else was convinced they were mutually supportive and all-inclusive, I was.

When it comes to being a professional, we see that a "Love your neighbor as yourself" mentality is critical to personal and organizational growth, to cultural security, and healthy societal contribution.

My level of inclination to invest in others and how freely and generously I do so speak volumes of the quality of my relationships . . . not to mention my capacity to actually be relational.

In turn, invested relationship cultivates emotional intelligence. Emotional soundness is partly supplied by healthy dieting habits and exercise. In return, emotional balance is energy and encouragement fueling strong health and wellness decisions. These priorities are all integrated.

Financial is no different. In fact, by the time we get to life priority number six we can assume that one through five are represented in how we handle number six.

Studies show that wealth has no correlation to happiness in either direction—it doesn't *make* a person happy or unhappy in the least. Money just gives you choices. It makes you more of what you already are.

Commit to being your very best in the first five areas and *Financial* will take care of itself, almost without fail. Who wants to be around you? Who wants to get behind you? Who is eager to see you succeed and be there to celebrate your success because of who you are, who you've become?

> One person, attracted to you because of whom you have become, can change your life forever!

Decide right now what small step you will take to further your spiritual wellness journey. What is your physical health worth? Do you have a *plan* in place to secure it to the best of your ability?

You are the average of the ten people with whom you spend the most time. Do your relationships reflect your values? What will it take to make them do so? What are you willing to do for emotional stability and peace of mind? What is your daily commitment to professional excellence?

What are the costs of financial freedom and the privilege of practicing generosity? Decide today how you will advance each of these priorities with some commitment. We are all writing our epitaph every day. Everyone we come in contact with is reading it.

Heading back to the airport, I had plenty of time, but my taxi driver was apparently unaware of that. He was driving considerably over the speed limit and rather recklessly. I informed him there was no hurry, but that had no effect.

Nearing the exit leading to the airport, I looked up and saw the traffic ahead was at a dead stop. My driver did not see this. In the back seat, directly behind him, some audible alarm I don't recall making must have gotten his attention just in time for him to swerve, barely missing the back end of a car at high speed. In doing so, he almost flipped us, putting our vehicle up on two wheels, then overcompensating the other way and on to the shoulder, swooping back in time to avoid leaving the highway. There was quite a bit more serpentine action before we were again stabilized and traveling in a straight line.

I can't recall the last time I raised my voice at someone. And never before had I yelled at a taxi driver. I did that day. "*Slooow Down!*" My heart was in my throat. *That* would have been one heck of a wreck!

Life is not a Journey to the grave
with the intention of
arriving safely in a pretty and well
preserved body,
but rather
to skid in sideways,
thoroughly worn out
and loudly proclaiming
"Wow, what a ride!"

—Peter Sage

CHAPTER 14

WONDER

10:00 AM, DAY 17, BRITISH AIRWAYS, FLIGHT 578

Over the Swiss Alps on the way to Venice, Italy—location of the final presentation of the tour—I looked out my window and saw, far below us, a little alpine village on the banks of a river cutting through the mountains. It was nestled between steep mountains, one of those point-and-shoot, can't-miss kind of places for anyone with a camera and a desire to create a scenic calendar.

I stared at it wonderingly. *What are those people doing; what are their lives like on this day?* Were they living with purpose; did they have plans, goals? Do they think of their lives in those terms? Were any of them looking up at the plane I was in, wondering?

There I was, a guy from Lake St. Louis, Missouri, flying to Venice to teach business people from London six-year goals . . . here are the tools, here are the principles. And down there in a little town . . . I wanted to know who, what, where? What was their approach?

Though I was not quite ready for the trip to be over, I was eager to reach the final city, the capper to all the presentations, the last Vistage group in this trip.

NOON, DAY 17, VENICE, ITALY, MARCO POLO AIRPORT

Venice . . . to attempt an acceptable description seems somewhat precocious. Even in my seventies I feel like a child just pondering the splendor of historic and magical that is Venice.

On the other hand, maybe words are the only way to convey anything near what it is like actually being there. Three days in Venice was a paradox: an awe-inspiring moment lost in wonder, where time either stopped or felt like a lifetime of its own—I'm not sure which; and yet, a tease . . . a glimpse into pure delight ended way too soon. Let's start with the more amusing beginning of the experience: the airport.

Arriving in Belfast made me wonder if I was part Irish, but I am pretty sure I have no Italian in me! From the moment I got off the plane, there was so much passion, so much animation that it felt to me like organized chaos, almost comical.

The reception was lavish; everyone was beyond friendly. But I had no idea what was going on. People pointed and called out orders or explanations or *something*. They dashed around and all sorts of busyness ensued.

Not understanding a word or possessing the ability to follow such gestures and body language, I simply had to trust others.

Does any of this include pairing me with my luggage or getting me to my hotel? I thought. Thankfully, it did, and all was well in hand. Before I knew it, I was on a boat—with luggage—and swept away into utter enchantment.

So, how did Venice come to be Venice? The answer is full of surprises, and absolutely nothing I would have expected.

To begin with, we have to create an imaginary model. Imagine a large inverted honeycomb in which the interior spaces—honey compartments—are solid. Well, somewhat solid . . . more like really dense wet sponge kind of solid. You've got a hundred and eighteen of those in different sizes and shapes. We'll call them "pieces" for the moment. Arrange the pieces on two sides of an S-like divide, a gap, with thinner gaps separating pieces from one another on both sides. What are solid wax walls of an actual honeycomb are opposite in our model—the gaps between the pieces.

We are now going to apply our arrangement to a larger model of the Mediterranean region. We submerge the arrangement in the shallow water of a lagoon just off the upper northeast mainland of Italy, so that all the gaps are now water-filled canals, some two hundred of them. The large, S-shaped one in the middle we will distinguish from the rest by the name Grand Canal. The spongy structures (our original "pieces") are islands. We cover the sponges with some moss, get it nice and soggy, and further imagine we've gone back in time to the early part of the fifth century.

That is Venice in its original, natural, and apparently uninhabitable state—one hundred and eighteen small, marshy islands spread across the northeast shore of Italy, the main clusters separated by canals.

This was most likely the condition of the islands for thousands of years of history—marsh fields, swamplands in a lagoon. If we were actually living in the fifth century, looking at the islands and imagining *forward*, nothing remotely constructive would occur to us concerning their future. But an interesting thing happened: necessity.

As the Roman Empire disintegrated, Huns and raiding Germanic bands (marauders, barbarians) swept down from the north, crushing everything in their path. Fleeing Roman citizens who made it safely as far as Italy's northeast coast had nowhere else to go but the swampy islands.

That's right: the original settlers of Venice were not real estate developers, architects, or engineers with grand visions for the most marvelous and romantic city in history—they were refugees motivated by terror. Who else would attempt to live in the disease-infested quagmire periodically submerged by high tide?

As things settled down a bit, the islanders, having come to think of the islands as *theirs*, decided to just go ahead and stay, and began devising ways to make squishiness homier. It was a challenge. But the nearby mainland was covered by hardwood forest (primarily oak), ideal for the kind of lumber needed to build up solid foundations from the small patches of watery properties.

Over time the forests of Italy's northeast coast were stripped bare (remaining so to this day) and the islands became interconnected platforms supporting building complexes.

By the time the islands began to appear valuable, the imperial baton of power had passed from Rome to Constantinople. The Byzantine Empire became the Venetians' primary trade focus, thus serving also as protector, helping to fend off Charlemagne's covetous ambitions in the eighth century, as well as all pirating interests. The result was recognition of Venice as a Byzantine territory by the ninth century, the beginning of its rise to world prominence.

Once created, Venice had other natural defenses, as it turned out. Island diseases, against which the islanders had developed immunities, were like a force field repelling would-be invaders. The thin island strip called Lido was positioned like a shield between Venice and the Adriatic Sea, protecting it from wind and waves. And the unique, isolated location of the city itself became an impenetrable position aiding its development into a naval and commercial juggernaut.

Throughout medieval times, Venice was a prominent city with no need of walls or gates. The original fleeing refugees had stumbled upon clusters of islands connected by a network of canals and waterways that happened to be natural conditions, ideally suited for trade and sea dominance throughout the Adriatic coast and across the eastern Mediterranean. At its peak, Venice boasted a naval prowess of over three thousand ships. It was a time when sea mastery meant wealth and fame.

Enjoying a monopoly of trade between Asia and northern Europe, Venice became the wealthiest city in the world during the Middle Ages. The superior grade of materials, excellence of foundational and structural masonry, and exquisite craftsmanship in every corner of the city were supplied by the wealth poured into it and a unified determination to build something extremely special, sound, and lasting.

Land surface was minuscule, so engineering was unavoidably prioritized by efficiency and ingenuity. "Venetian" became a peculiar character recalling international influences and centuries of development (Gothic, Arabic, Byzantine, Renaissance, Baroque). And close foundational ties with the East have always defined Venetian charm.

The discovery of the New World by Columbus changed the dynamics of international focus, relations, trade, and enterprise. Smitten by colonization fever, foreign resources ramped up naval power and imperial ambitions. Lacking a vision for such things—why would anyone living in the world's most beautiful city care to plant a flag anywhere else?—the Republic of Venice got left behind in the power scramble.

The fifteenth century marked the beginning decline of Venetian trade dominance and military might. Venice enjoyed a more aesthetic prominence and influence in the Renaissance, and it had independence until the end of the eighteenth century when Napoleon Bonaparte finally conquered it. After a brief stint as property of Austria, inclusion with a unified Italy brought Venice into the modern era where it thrives in yet another kind of prominence: one of the world's premier tourist destinations.

Eight of us rode an open speedboat toward an island totally dedicated to the resort at which I was staying and where the presentation would occur the following day. As you float into Venice in complete awe, it is impossible to fathom its unintentional beginnings. I don't believe I have ever stared so entranced for so long.

Buildings and walkways covered the resort island. After checking in, I took a jog around the island, needing to release some awe-stimulated endorphins.

What an extraordinary place! I thought, turning on the path that resulted in the next fifty yards of my jog being aimed directly at the causeway connecting Venice to the mainland.

I felt tempted to pinch myself and make sure this was real. I would feel that sensation frequently over the next few days.

While running, I stared across the water at the gleaming, sun-lit city. The middle of nowhere isolation, obscurity . . . humble (maybe even undesirable) beginnings; the whole unexpected takeoff of the truly exceptional journey—impetus of necessity; driven from comfort and security by some greater force; bold, courageous decisions meeting with uncanny placements and timing; overarching help, encourage-ment, guiding influence, and protection; rise to prominence and wealth; international relationships of incalculable value in resource and benevolence; shift from ascending greatness to focus on inspiration—"renaissance"—and then to great reach of magnetism, association, interaction . . . *appeal*.

I was just a kid on a farm twenty minutes from the nearest *telephone*. Learning to fly was necessary because of turkey delivery demands. . . . As if I could place my own story as a template over that of the marvel before me, there was a peculiarity of wonder, of resonance deep in my soul.

Even *this* . . . I did not plan this. It was added after the original itiner-ary was set, by the London Vistage folks—something they wanted to do as a culmination of the tour.

Following the run, I barely touched a light lunch—the effect of excite-ment on my appetite. It was time to hail a boat at the dock and head for Grand Canal.

Though only about a hundred of the man-powered, colorfully stylized gondolas that once dominated the waters remain, boats are ubiquitous in Venice and the surrounding lagoon and distant sea entrance—ocean liners, yachts, motorboats. . . .

The city's public transit system is a fleet of motorized bus-boats. Taxis, food and laundry pickup, and delivery, emergency fire and ambulance services, trash collection, and mail service are all by boat. As motorized vehicles are outlawed, "streets" are narrow pedestrian walking paths, connectors, and generally crowded. All travel is by boat or foot.

Still displaying the booty of medieval sea ventures and treasures of a grand carnival of international trade, Venice is a kind of architectural trophy case. And not an inch is wasted.

Decorum, order, design, and attention to detail are pure eye candy. Painted signs on every corner direct visitors to wherever they want to go. Every building has an address displayed in red letters surrounded by a black oval background; and the addresses relate to districts as opposed to streets.

These are only matters of convenience, as getting lost in such a place is not actually *lost*, just a temporary disruption of intention. Being on an island where you can't get off is actually perfect for wandering aimlessly, allowing time and agenda to be forgotten. But wandering in a gondola, your driver singing to you in Italian ... *that* is dream-like.

In their heyday, Venetians had no inclination to handle their wealth discretely. The more lavish the display the better. Stark white is contrasted by brightly colored surfaces of red, blue, and yellow, often boldly trimmed in black.

Recalling its long history of great wealth and possibly its most striking impression, Venice is a city of palaces. (I am told they were once frescoed in stunning colors trimmed in gold leaf.) They line Grand Canal and are only outnumbered by boats and people.

The historical ambience was sensually delicious. St. Marks Basilica, built in the eleventh century ... well, I had the boatman pass by it from every possible vantage point over and over. It alone made my experience feel like time travel and a visit to Byzantium. A clock tower in St. Mark's Square was built in the mid-1400s.

Everywhere I looked deep history stared back at me. Portions of art collections in the city *begin* at the Middle Ages and move up through the eighteenth century. Ordinances protect the city's medieval origins, banning any alterations so future visitors can have the same experience as I had.

The oldest inhabited island, Torcello, is where mainland refugees originally settled. For some reason, it is the least developed, allowing for an appreciation of the natural condition of the islands—mostly brush-covered and marshy.

It appeared as though 80 percent of the tourists were aware of 20 percent of the city. But every bit of it was dazzling to my eyes. Not the least of which was the clear blue water and the reflections dancing upon it. Every now and then it seemed Venice was a fluid contemplation of water, light, stone, space, and time. That temptation to pinch myself returned again and again. Having spent the afternoon exhausting my capacity of wonder, I realized it was time to get back to the resort where I was to meet the Vistage members for dinner.

Why do children love to
hide and seek?
Ask any person who has a passion
to explore
and discover and create.
The choice to hide so many wonders
from you
is an act of love
that is a gift
inside the process of life.

—William Paul Young, *The Shack*

CHAPTER 15

FRIENDS

6:00 PM, DAY 17, SAN CLEMENTE PALACE HOTEL, VENICE

Rapport is a phenomenon, not an achievement. If you have ever experienced connection that seemed preceded by affinity, feel free to fill in between the lines. The group from London Vistage meeting in Venice was all men, and it was as if I had planned a retreat with my own band of brothers.

We all got into a boat and headed for St. Mark's Basilica. It always adds something important to the experience when you see the spectacular with someone else. I quickly realized I was the only one visiting Venice for the first time, as the others provided information, history, and anecdotal humor about the famous city.

From the Basilica we headed to St. Mark's Square, where we enjoyed a five-course meal. Listening to the stories, opinions, and commentaries revealing more of each of my new friends' personalities was the best part. Afterward, a lengthy walk burned off some of the calories from the feast before we ended up at Café Florian, where we parked for hours, talking and observing Venice nightlife.

Outside, under a clear sky, the stars were brightly arrayed against the background of infinite dark. But the buildings and walkways twinkled, adorned with innumerable lights, reflections upon shiny surfaces, and flashes of cameras. A baroque ensemble was near, escorting our imaginations into Venice's own special version of dreamland. Everywhere, people danced and sang—not necessarily to what *our* musicians were playing. It was a magical atmosphere.

Interrupting all of that—perhaps inspired by it—one of our company leaned over and asked, "What do you think is the greatest evidence of mental and emotional health?"

I had almost forgotten I was the speaker at a Vistage retreat and had been enjoying, at least for the evening, *not* being the primary focus of speaking. Listening to everyone else and being the guest was relaxing and entertaining. So, the question seemed to come from out of nowhere.

Scanning Venice's abundant animations of happiness and beauty, perhaps he expected a painter's answer—something about dancing, laughter, companionship, music, partying. Only one thing came to mind, and it was not far from any of those.

"The readiness to celebrate another person's success," I answered.

He smiled, raised his wine glass in my direction, and said, "Hear, hear!"

It caught the attention and curiosity of some of the others with us, who could not have heard a previous word over the music. He leaned over again and offered his own contribution to my short answer. "If someone I know is doing well, experiencing great success . . . and I say, the more the better, even if it blows away anything I have ever done. . . ." He paused, thoughtful for a moment. "It can make me feel giddy, so that I break into laughter."

The interaction left me pleasantly contemplative for several minutes, as the recent reports of great strides and breakthroughs of several friends back home ran through my mind.

David Adams, the group chair, may or may not have overheard the conversation, but he asked how the present location and company compared to people and places that occupy my time back home (or, at least, that's what I interpreted from hearing about every other word clearly). I had the distinct feeling they were conspiring to get to know the Tom Hill that did *not* come prepared.

My answer began with a short and obvious, "There is nothing to compare with Venice." The second part of my answer was just the opposite.

"As far as the people I spend time with . . . very similar." I included an explanation:

> I really believe we are each the average of the ten people we spend the most time with. So I tend to gravitate toward people whose abilities are far superior to my own, at least in some major area I really care about.
>
> I have friends much like you guys, who are financially astute in ways that continually educate me. I know people with huge hearts for the ordinary anybody, something I have to work at and am encouraged to do so by our friendships. I make efforts to be in the company of visionaries, because I am not one. I'm drawn to CEO types, those rare and remarkable people gifted in engineering and leadership who home in on exact organizational needs and apply know-how to making solutions happen *right now*.
>
> For a person traveling around hoping to inspire others, it is especially important for me to know someone who is way better than me at it. My friend Tammy Fadler, for example, is a natural-born inspiration with a lot of practice and intentionality added to what she started with. Her book, *Finding the Pearl*, is her story of immigration to the US from Vietnam as a young lady on just $10. Wow, what a story! And, of course, my wife, Betty . . . she has the heart of a lion and then some; she has a *lion pride* of courage.
>
> I am *upped* by associating with all of these very different types of people. More important, I love them and they love me. That alone makes me a better person.
>
> But the main targets, as far as my intentions are concerned, are generous people. That is a quality of influence I could never get too much of.

The last comment launched a savory dialogue among the group, each man sharing some of the details of philanthropic endeavors in their own lives. Somewhere along the way, I realized the conversation was about power—real power. We were a bunch of ordinary guys privileged to sit around in casual conversation about the power to change the world.

This is what I know of the wealthy. Some would say otherwise, contending that wealth is built on greed and selfishness and such. I guess I don't know where those people live, because I never seem to meet them. The mark of everyone I know to be living the exceptional life is generous *giving*. I enjoy success, but I know this: it's not about me. If I ever forget it, I have plenty of examples to steer me back toward generosity.

Friendship is
a strong habitual
inclination
in two persons
to promote
the good and happiness
of another.

—Eustace Budgell

CHAPTER 16

POSSIBILITY

From the very beginning, openness and an uncommon sense of possibility propelled a daylong movement of total engagement. The group had the synergy of shared anticipation concerning the power of strategy. Generosity of invitation made for easy access to each man's wealth of experience and insight. All were equally active as listeners and speakers. They separated into smaller groups for workshop activities; into pairs for writing and sharing goals; going solo for vision and commitment journaling; and coming back together for group input and brainstorming.

Everything was in the old-fashioned, "jump in head first" style. The day glided by and, *quite suddenly* it felt, I brought the final presentation and the entire tour to a conclusion with some closing comments.

> Success in life really comes down to positive mental attitude. You are what you think. If I recall correctly, Henry Ford said, "If you believe you can, you are right. And if you believe you can't, you are right."

> If you get that, the rest of this is superfluous . . . just a good excuse for a really great three-day vacation getaway with friends. Beyond it I have only one other thing to say:

> Today is the day!

> I live every day of my life with that same propulsion of possibility. I know each of you do also. Today is the day of

possibility, the gift God has personally made and given to me. Right there is motivation galore.

Today is the day I realize possibility. Today is the day I invest in possibilities with other people's names on them. Today is its own opportunity, the day I make the most of possibility in the form of someone else's blessing.

Today is the day I *see* possibility. Just look around . . . what else would I do? This is life! This is possibility. This is my exceptional life . . . blessed beyond measure!

If you do not take another thing away from this wonderful time together, my friends, remember this . . . I deliver it to you with all the love, conviction, and urgency my heart can muster:

Today is the day!

Three Miles High On A Snow Covered Peak
He Unfurls His Wings And He Is Free
Alone At Dawn While The Rest Of The World
Is Still Fast Asleep He Is Soaring

Where The Wind And The Sky Collide
There Is The Place You Will Find Him
Born With A Passion—A Dream In His Heart
He Cries, "I Am An Eagle—And I Fly . . ."

Deep Inside I Know That God
Placed Me On This Earth For A Reason
Awake My Soul The Time Is At Hand
I Will Find The Courage To Rise Above

Where The Joy Inside Me Comes To Life
That's Where Believers Will Find Me
Born With A Passion—A Dream In My Heart
Say I, "I Am An Eagle!—And I Fly . . ."

—Mickey Olsen, Tammy Fadler, *I Am an Eagle!*

EPILOGUE

Taxiing toward our runway in Dallas and the flight back to St. Louis, I witnessed something few passengers ever see. Out at the entry to gates along the C concourse, two fire engines faced one another at a distance of about fifty yards. Great streams of water shooting into the air and at one another from mounted hoses atop both emergency vehicles formed an arch through which a 757 was passing. It was a retirement salute. The pilot of the plane had just completed the final flight of his career and was heading toward a docking station where he would deliver one last load of passengers safely to their destination.

The sight also seemed symbolic. Retirement was the mode I was anticipating, as if passing through seven cities and five countries in three weeks had been my farewell salute to the rigors of professional life and accomplishment. Betty was still recovering from her stroke, which continued to be a significant life adjustment for both of us. An escalation of activities and impact was not on my radar.

But, as a friend once told me: "If you want to give God a good laugh, just tell him your plans."

Well, I did. And they looked like hobbies. Forty to fifty speeches a year, forty Executive Coaching clients (known as "Hill's Angels"), my weekly newsletter, the *Eaglezine*, and three Eagle Summit events annually made up a cruise control lifestyle that was about to change with just a few surprise introductions.

It all began one night when I woke up to a clear voice at 4:30 in the morning telling me, "Tom, you are going to touch a million lives."

Soon afterward a friend and Goalden Eagle client, Missy Palitzsch, told me I needed to meet a fellow named Gary Baker. Gary and I live near each other, so it was easy to make that happen. I met him on a Monday at his restaurant, Donatelli's. We were not long into conversation—sharing some of the usual background and career information—before he expressed some rather significant enthusiasm about our introduction.

"I can't believe I am meeting you and that you live just minutes away from me," he said. "I've been praying for a way to help my clients with all areas of their lives, concerns I know them to have but that fall outside my business of financial advisory. Here you are doing just that, providing people with insight on how to achieve a proper balance in all those areas of life they care most about."

Gary had recently met a man at a retreat hosted by his firm. He arrived at the event a little early and saw the man—who had some evident physical challenges—setting up some audio-video equipment. Gary thought about how great it was that a man with such physical challenges could work the audio-video table. To his great surprise, he discovered this "audio-video" guy was the speaker for the day. His name was John O'Leary. Even more surprising, John would be the most inspiring speaker Gary had ever heard.

After relating these things to me, he said, "I want you to meet John O'Leary."

That Wednesday, a friend of mine in North Carolina, Steve Miller, called and said, "Tom, I have just heard the greatest speaker I have ever heard. Totally life-changing experience! His name is John O'Leary, and he lives right there in St. Louis. You've got to meet him."

Saturday of the same week, Betty and I were in Keokuk, Iowa, to attend my brother's engagement party. I got up and went to the hotel lobby to get a local paper and a cup of coffee. There on page three is a picture of John O'Leary. He had just given a talk at a school in Keokuk.

I said, "God ... OK, I get it. I'll make it a priority to meet this John O'Leary as soon as I get back home."

When I met John I was awed by his story and impressed by his passion for encouraging others. John was caught in a house fire that he accidentally started when he was nine years old and was severely burned over 90 percent of his body. Given less than a 1 percent chance of surviving, and having no desire to face the anguish of living, a series of miracles and love encounters—ordinary folks giving of themselves in extraordinary ways—moved John from breath to breath, then day to day until he left the hospital months later to face a radically altered life.

Inspired by the kindness and generosity of others, John believed in the value of his life and kept fighting. Now a graduate of St. Louis University, business owner, husband, and father of four, he travels the world passing on the inspiration he received.

Before I knew it, Gary and John were joining me on a speaking trip to Kansas City, and we were figuring out ways to work together. I shared with Gary my fifty-two coaching lessons. Soon afterward he came to me and said, "I have an idea. What do you think of putting all this together in a cohesive, interactive package and calling it the Tom Hill Institute?"

I thought to myself, *This sounds a lot like a major leap out of cruise control.* But what I said was, "I'm all for it if you put it together—the infrastructure, the strategy, the technology, everything. I am yours 100 percent until midnight on June 30, 2014. That's our time frame for seeing if we can make it work."

More adventures in serendipity brought Dan Kraus to our growing THI family. Formerly a top tier Anheuser-Busch executive, Dan managed the company's five billion dollar pension fund, global cash management and capital spending. The InBev takeover provided Dan the nudge he needed to tackle his "second-half" passion, helping others achieve financial freedom. He was building a new wealth management business, which was personally and professionally stretching, when he met Gary Baker and bought into the THI vision.

Soon Dan was a part of THI strategic planning. He brought to the team a completely different frame of reference—that of executive suite organizational comprehension. His ability to take Gary's vision and make it structurally sound, functional, and operational was immediately evident.

I had the network, the Eagle platform, but had no vision for doing anything more with it. Gary had the vision I lacked. Dan is like the "engineer" building infrastructure. Thankfully, they both had more than just talent and vision. They had commitment. And as a result, we launched the fifty-two (every Monday morning at 7:00) lessons on January 1, 2013, with five thousand participants in fifty states, fifteen countries, and one-hundred-twenty companies. I have a sense we are on the front end of some true soaring. From the beginning, everything about THI has been moved along by individuals recognizing the importance of what others bring to the table. It continues to expand by that simple formula.

An Eagle Summit in Park City, Utah, was attended by a new Hill's Angel, who thought it would be a great opportunity to introduce Christine Hassler, a terrific speaker and leadership motivator. Impressed by her presentation, Gary pulled Christine aside and they talked for an hour or so about a vision for Emerging Leaders Organization (ELO). It has become another action plan under the THI umbrella. I brought the people together in Park City. A suggestion led to Christine being one of the event speakers. Christine made an impact that inspired Gary to cook up a vision for expansion. Not one of us went to Park City with anything remotely related to an ELO concept on our minds, I least of all. At seventy-six I was not prepared to be thinking like a Gen-X.

By similar means, other pieces of the THI puzzle have found their places. An event came together where we brought in thirty-six speakers to each record a fifteen-minute segment over a thirty-six-hour period of time at a local university. We called it "36X36" and the THI Speakers Bureau was launched. Hill's Angels—where it all began—has added HPA (High Performance Advisors), a coaching certification program under the direction of Dr. Roger Hall. And connection with Opportunity International (a micro lending charitable organization enabling individuals in third-world nations to become financially independent) and God Cares (serving returning veterans) are integrated benevolence relationships of increasing importance.

So much for retirement! Yet, as cruise control was transformed into exponential growth, where the essentials were concerned, nothing changed. Each development along the way has continued to support a prioritization of personal growth—spiritual, emotional, physical, relational, professional, and financial—moved along by G-curves and tipping points toward multiplication of people living the exceptional life!

MASTER ACTION LIST
CHAPTER-BY-CHAPTER

So we've had this wonderful time together. But, did you really think you would get by that easy? One action list well executed will change your life forever—this one!

Chapter One—One of the signature habits of highly accomplished people is a daily checklist. Commit to making a checklist every day. Do not get discouraged if you do not perfectly complete everything on your list every day. Establishing the habit of a daily action list is its own worthy accomplishment.

Chapter Two—Discipline is *doing things you know you should do until they become a habit*. And discipline = *OIMF!* (the Odds In My Favor). Identify one thing you know you should do—that thing you often lament not doing—that you have not been doing and commit to doing it starting now.

Chapter Three—What's next? The past is behind you. What is it you want to accomplish next? Get bold and name it. Name its three most significant obstacles—those the naysayers would point to when making a case for how unlikely it is for you to do this.

> *Chapter three bonus assignment:* You have that miracle moment (everyone does, by whatever name), the thing you're not comfortable talking about. Talk about it. Start sharing it with others whenever appropriate. It will do your soul good to hear the report, to be reminded that you believe it was not a fluke, no mere coincidence—something special happened because you are special.

Chapter Four—How a day is begun is of critical importance. What one thing will you commit to doing to start each day well?

Chapter Five—Name one *little* thing you will do every day to bless someone with whom you come in contact.

Chapter Six—Where do you envision yourself six years from today? Writing it down is a fun first step in being intentional about it. Create a written vision for where you want to be (spiritually, physically, relationally, emotionally, professionally, and financially) eighteen months, three years, and six years from now.

Chapter Seven—We all have different interests, of course. They are the raw materials of shared memories. The idea of climbing all the "Fourteeners" in Colorado inspired me to create some incredible memories with my son, Scott. Is there an idea that causes you to respond, "Wow, that seems like it would be a lot of fun!"? Admit you *want* to do it, decide you are *going* to do it, and pick someone with whom you will plan, prepare, and do it together. When you and your partner have successfully turned that idea into experience and memory, pick another and do the same.

Chapter Eight—My mud puddle moment was truly a low point. I responded by changing my clothes (albeit, while grumbling) and going out into the rainy day to try and make something happen. Even then I got lost. But the kind person I met when just trying to get directions took an interest in what I was doing, which led to a sale, one of the first successes of my RE/MAX journey. Betty rejoined me a short time later, and I was attitude-adjusted, encouraged, and bolstered by resolve to move forward. Who do you know to be experiencing a mud puddle moment this week? Figure out some small way to encourage or support them. Look around for someone else face down in a puddle next week and make the effort to lend a hand, listen with genuine interest, or share a kind word. Make being an encourager a habit.

Chapter Nine—What do you want to accomplish more than anything else? Create one master goal for getting it done and develop a plan of execution for that goal, including identification of essential tasks, necessary skills development, important relationship building, and obstacles that must be overcome.

Chapter Ten—Add to your master goal plan a time determination for each of its component parts. This in effect converts all aspects of the plan into measurable goals supporting the primary goal. You will find you have created a map for the uncharted territory. Following the map is taking your goal seriously and taking *you* having a goal seriously. You have somewhere you want to go. Following the map will get you there.

Chapter Eleven—My RE/MAX journey was launched by decisions most thought were ludicrous. Turning my back on status, stability, and security, on many occasions the man in the mirror was the most critical, the biggest bully trying to get me to back down. Yet, the challenges along the way led to resolve and discovery of the authentic person inside. Write out the story of your biggest success to date. Write an evaluation of all the things the story reports about who you are.

Chapter Twelve—Failure is critical. People who dream and pursue big dreams naturally face challenges and experience failures along the way. Make a list of three of your heroes. Do some research and further list their biggest failures. Meet with a friend and discuss what the failures say about those heroes and how they relate to their accomplishments. Here's the fun part. Share some of your own failures in pursuing dreams and discuss what they speak of you. The order is important: heroes and their failures first, then you and yours. Next, go back to your goals plan and circle everything that is *too* safe. Make adjustments in the direction of risking failure.

Chapter Thirteen—The exceptional life majors on serving others—a "Love your neighbor as yourself" moral obligation. Commit to serve somebody in some specific way outside of the norm of your daily routine once a week.

Chapter Fourteen—Adventure is the spice of life. Wonder is life at its surprising, savory best. Here is the most fun you will ever receive in the form of an assignment: commit to a one-day adventure once a month (eight hours minimum). Go somewhere you've never been, do something you've never done, explore something you find intriguing, go wherever wonder leads, treat yourself to something that inspires questions you have never asked.

Chapter Fifteen—Friendship is habitual, reciprocal goodwill. Indulge it, spread it, invest in it, populate your life with it, once a day practice it—make the phone call, send the note.

Chapter Sixteen—Choose an accountability partner as a witness to your application of signature and date to this eighteen-month action list commitment. Invite them to hold you to it. Today is the day!

HILL

My great, great ... grandfather, William Hill, and his brother, Thomas, sailed across the Atlantic and disembarked on the James River to settle in the land that is now Virginia, having left behind their hometown of Shrewsbury (above), in west central England.

This statue of General Ambrose Powell
Hill stands at an intersection in Richmond,
Virginia. General A P Hill was the cousin of
my grandfather's grandfather, Thomas Henry
Hill, who moved to Missouri in 1848, and
after whom I was named. General Hill was
one of the greatest of the confederate generals
during the Civil War. After Lee surrendered
to Grant, word of the war's end took some
time to get around. General Hill made it
through the entire war alive, but while riding
across an open field was shot dead by a Union
sniper who did not know the war was over.
He was buried in Hollywood Cemetery in
Richmond and was dug up for the making of
this statue.

My teacher and our entire class, grades one through eight.

"Rainy Day" was my daily transportation to school.

On my Harley

With my son, Scott, atop Mount Torrey in Colorado

Crossing the finish line of a marathon in Greece

Looking down at the Alps on the way to Venice. If you look real close you can see a tiny town nestled between the mountains. Somewhere down there people were living a different life, going about things a different way than I have ever considered . . . or, who knows, maybe not so different at all. It's a big wonderful world.

My favorite picture of Betty: on top of a
mountain in Eza, France.